Lost Daughters
Writing Adoption From a Place of Empowerment and Peace

Edited By

Amanda H.L. Transue-Woolston
Julie Stromberg
Karen Pickell
Jennifer Anastasi

Published by,
CQT Media And Publishing, and
LGA Inc.

Edited By: Amanda H.L. Transue-Woolston, Julie Stromberg
Karen Pickell, Jennifer Anastasi

Cover Artwork by Carlynne Hershberger

ISBN-13: 978-0-9885858-4-3

"You are beautiful and strong. Live with courage and authenticity. May your roots continue to deepen and ground your spirit with an unshakable knowing of who you are and what your purpose is despite life's storms. Carry in your heart those who have been a part of your past, cherish those who are beside you in the present, and surround yourself with people who believe in you and are willing to walk alongside you in the future. Remember, true beauty does not come from outward adornment; it comes when you illuminate that which is within. May the beauty of your presence and soul's light continue to shine for others each step of the way."

Your Journey Matters

—Stephanie Kripa Cooper-Lewter, Ph.D., L.M.S.W., from her doctoral dissertation, *Identity Journeys: Life Stories of Women Adopted Transnationally as Children*

4

Table of Contents

5

Trials & Triumph 95

About the Authors and Editors 145

Founder's Preface

This anthology is a collection of writings by the authors of the Lost Daughters blog. Lost Daughters is an independent, collaborative writing project that I founded in 2011 in an effort to give an accessible writing platform for adopted women. Boasting nearly 30 authors at this time, Lost Daughters is written and edited entirely by adopted women, several of whom balance multiple roles in adoption and foster care along with being adopted. The blog's name was inspired by author and adoptee B.J. Lifton's concept of one's self becoming lost and found throughout the experience of being adopted.

Our mission is to bring readers the perspectives and narratives of adopted women, and to highlight their strength, resiliency, and wisdom. We aim to critically discuss the positives and negatives of the adoption institution from a place of empowerment and peace.

Our authors come from all walks of life and have a variety of worldviews, religions, political stances, types of adoption, countries of origin, and countries of residence. Our ages span early 20s to late 60s. Although we cannot possibly cover every experience and perspective of adoptees in this book or on our blog, we try our best to provide insight on what it is like to live adoption from the adoptee perspective. The biographical statements of each author have been provided at the end of this book for the purpose of contextualization.

We do not pour our hearts and souls into the blog or this subsequent book in order to tell readers how to feel about adoption. We do not view it as our role or function to dictate as a group what particular stances on adoption issues we believe the world should have. We hold one principal as always true: the voices of adult adoptees make adoption better.

We hope that each author's unique and diverse viewpoint will give readers something to think about. The adoption community has long given an imbalanced proportion of focus on the pre-adoption period and the actual event of the adoption. The inadequate attention to post-adoption needs and support has subsequently impacted adoption policies and what services are offered as far as adoption practice is concerned. We hope to make a change in this area of adoption's culture by raising our voices as women who have adoption as an intersecting variable across the many aspects of life and identity.

I thank you for reading this book and joining us on this incredible journey.

Amanda H.L. Transue-Woolston, B.S.W.
Founding Editor, Lost Daughters

Introduction: The Sisterhood of Adopted Women

By Julie Stromberg

"You know what the secret is? It's so simple. We love one another. We're nice to one another. Do you know how rare that is?"

—Carmen, in *The Sisterhood of the Traveling* Pants by Ann Brashares

Early into the Lost Daughters blog project, I had the privilege and honor of spending time out in the actual world with one of my fellow Lost Daughters. It was our first time meeting in person despite knowing each other online for many months. And we did something that normal women do all the time—ate lunch and went shopping.

What struck me during our outing was how comfortable I felt in her presence. We discussed all kinds of topics, from motherhood to career to religion and, yes, adoption. The connection and sense of camaraderie was wonderful because for the first time in my life, I was able to exist in my entirety as an adopted woman.

The more we chatted, the more I realized how, for me, the typical conversations women have when getting to know each other often end up being tempered somewhat because I don't feel free to let my adopted woman out. It is sometimes difficult for me to make small talk about such seemingly inane topics, such as where I grew up or where my family lives, because there is an

10

underlying current to subjects such as these to which non-adopted women can't relate.

It was so freeing for this not to be the case because I was lunching and shopping with another adopted woman. We threw out terminology that mere mortals wouldn't use. I was able to say "my n-dad said this" or "my a-mom did this" with relish because my companion spoke the same language. I didn't have to explain how adoption played into anything because she already knew. I didn't have to temper myself at all. Spending time with her was like letting out a huge sigh of relief after the airplane has landed safely on solid ground.

The experience got me thinking about us as adopted women, about how our experiences influence the way we maneuver through life and exist in the world. Throughout history, women often have been expected to be demure and obedient, understated, and accepting. This expectation has changed a lot over time, except for adopted women. No doubt, our adoptions have impacted how we relate to other women, how we might approach motherhood, and how we present ourselves within society at large. Yet we are still expected to be grateful, accepting and quiet when it comes to this huge part of who we are as women.

Time to shatter those expectations, ladies. Together, we are strong. We are a Sisterhood of Adopted Women. And we don't have to be quiet or demure.

Identity

Middle School Math: Asian + Oriental + Chink = Run

By Mila C. Konomos

To any white friends I made during middle school, I was their "little Chinese friend," except for the obvious fact that I was not actually Chinese.

"But it's all the same, right? You're all Asian, right?"

"Sure, we're all Asian, but it's kind of like you're all white, but you're not the same white as the white people in England or Australia or Ireland, or something like that."

"What does it matter anyway? Korean, Chinese, who cares?"Just as Alice finished her sentence, I suddenly felt something first hit me in the back and then in the back of my head."

I turned around.

"Hey, you Oriental! Hey, Chink! Do you understand that?"

Alice ran away.

I felt a bit disoriented. I heard cackling and raucous laughter. I was trying to figure out what was happening when I felt another object hit me in the forehead. I looked down the hill and saw a group of three boys laughing and pointing. One of the boys had a giant soda cup. He reached in and pulled out a piece of ice. At the same time, I saw one of the other boys pick up a rock. They both began to throw their found objects in my direction.

A part of me stood there in disbelief, not wanting to comprehend what was transpiring. I didn't want to believe that this was actually happening to me.

13

Finally, I realized that they were indeed throwing rocks and pieces of ice at me.

Move your legs and feet, you dummy. Get out of the way. Do something. Don't just stand there like you're some kind of idiot.

I turned back around and started running with my head down, trying to cover it with my notebook. I thought to myself, surely this is a mistake. Surely, I'm having a bad dream. But the throbbing at the back of my head told me that this was anything but a dream.

I stopped for a second to look back again. I had made it over the crest of the hill. I couldn't see the boys anymore, which hopefully meant that they couldn't see me either. Maybe it was all a misunderstanding. Maybe I misheard what they said.

The street ended at the top of the hill where it met with the street on which I lived. I took a left. Just two houses down on the left, I reached my house. I made my way up the driveway. I got to the front door and dug out my house key from my backpack.

I paused. This is my home, right? I looked around at the yard and the front of the house.

I unlocked the front door. It cracked open; the alarm was beeping. I keyed in the code. No one else was home.

I made my way up the stairs to my bedroom. When I reached the top of the stairs, I examined the arrangement of family photos perched atop one of the cabinets. I wanted to take them all down and bring them to school, so that everyone could see that I was just like they were. I'm the same. See, my family looks just like yours.

I got to my bedroom and closed the door. I put my book bag down.

I stood in front of my full-length mirror. I turned to the side and then back, facing forward. Every time I saw myself, I was still surprised to see this short, black-haired, almond-eyed girl staring back.

* * *

But the world never forgets what it sees. And the world does its best to make certain that I, too, will never forget the way it sees me.

* * *

Alice and I never talked after that incident, which clarified that what had taken place that day had not been a bad dream or a mistake.

I never told anyone about what happened; I hoped that pretending as though it never happened would make it hurt less.

My mom eventually asked me about Alice. I told her that I didn't like Alice anymore, that she wasn't a nice friend. My mom didn't ask me any other questions. She simply said, "I'm sorry. Well, don't worry, Honey, there are more nice friends out there to be made. Don't worry yourself over the duds."

I wanted to say in response, "What if I'm one of the duds?" But instead, I just gave her a smile and said, "Thanks, Mom."

Lifetime Secrets and Their Effect on the Adoptee

By Susan Perry

As an older adopted person, I've come to terms with the fact that there are many facts about my background I'll probably never know. While I've had a sweet, but brief conversation with my first mother by phone, I've never laid eyes on her, and she didn't wish to meet face to face. I don't know the name of my original father, although social workers at the agency that placed me in 1950 do. My first mother said that she couldn't tell me anything about him "because he was a married man." As a woman in her eighties, this was still her thinking, I suppose, that she did something terribly wrong by becoming entangled in an improper relationship.

My understanding from my "non-identifying information" is that my first father was a family friend from Denmark—both my original parents are Danish—who was separated from his wife at the time of his relationship with my first mother. My original mother, I am told, hoped for a long-term commitment; my original father, quite a bit older at the time of my conception—age 53—was apparently unwilling to commit.

I am told by an agency social worker that there was some talk of me going to live with my first father's son and wife before I was placed for adoption. I still have no idea where I was during the first three months of my life or who cared for me during that time. I realize that I know a lot more than some adopted people do. I know my ancestry. I know my first father lived into his 80s and that my first mother is still alive at the age of 89. I know I have a half-sister who is five years older than I am, and, at some point, I'll probably contact her.

I believe that I have all the information about my first mother that I am going to get from her; she made it clear that she did not wish to talk again. She was able to tell me in that brief phone conversation that "she loved me in her heart," but she has lived her entire life not acknowledging my existence to anyone else except for her own mother.

It irritates me to no end that I can't learn more about my first father, as he sounds very interesting. He was raised in Denmark, trained as a pilot, and loved the outdoor life, just as I always have. He is long deceased, as is his son, so just what risk there would be for the agency to release his name to me is hard to understand. And that is the injustice and the ludicrous nature of sealed record laws. In this case, they afford more rights to the dead than they do to the living, and they bind the adopted person to a lifetime restraining order.

Although the sealed record system encourages denial as a standard coping mechanism, I think both my first mother and my adoptive mother were just starting to understand the complexities and the hidden nature of adoption as they both approached their old age. My first mother picked up the phone and called me after we had exchanged letters and medical information, I believe, because she came to realize that in protecting her own secret and rejecting my offer to

17

meet, she was hurting me at a core and primal level. She wasn't able to open up completely, but she was able to say "I love you," and I appreciate the fact that she was at least able to reach out a little. She relinquished, after all, in a very different era from the open society in which we now live.

And while my adoptive mother didn't like to think about the fact that I had an original family, she did say to me as she grew older, "If you ever want to know more, the files are right there in that drawer." She herself knew nothing about sealed records, and my adoption decree included my original birth name. My mother only knew that adoption had worked extremely well for her—it had given her the family she so badly wanted. But I think she felt deep inside that there was an underlying, hidden aspect. She was aware that there were other people in the world to whom I was connected. She just didn't want to go there herself, and she had no idea how often my interior thoughts had turned to my ancestors. Who were they, and what was my story?"

One thing I do know for sure is that my adoptive parents truly did love me, and that love and support has helped to make me the person I am today. My genes have helped to make me that person as well, and it's only natural from my perspective that I should want to know more about the people who passed them on to me. I am motivated to write about adoption issues because I believe strongly that sealed records are unjust, and that they are truly damaging to many, many people. They encourage unhealthy thinking, repression, and denial as the means for coping with life.

In my case, sealed records were the reason it took me too long to grow up and assume total responsibility for my own life. In a way, sealed records imprisoned me because I didn't feel free to express my innermost feelings about adoption. Although I seemed to be successful in my personal and professional life—I did well in school, earned graduate degrees, married happily, had children, and worked as a teacher and public relations professional—I did not feel empowered to take charge of my own story until I was well into my 40s.

Every adopted person's journey is unique, but I know that my story is not atypical. I just cannot understand why, as a culture, we would continue to shackle adopted people to an institution that is governed by such archaic and repressive laws when the data tells us clearly that most first mothers are open to contact. Those who are not, like my original mother, can simply say no. This is an emotional subject for sure, but all of us affected are adults now—we do not need outside agents supervising our own, very personal business.

The repressive laws set the tone for the either/or thinking we often see in online responses to adoption articles. The kind of thinking that assumes those adoptees who search are expressing disloyalty to their adoptive parents, or that the adoptee should just "be grateful" and move on. These attitudes are hurtful and dismissive of many adopted people's experiences when the reality is that an adoptee does have two sets of parents, and like every other human being, is a unique mix of her DNA and upbringing.

Telling adoptees that they are not entitled by

law to access their own original birth certificates is belittling and unfair when every other American citizen can apply for and secure hers for a nominal fee. It is institutional discrimination, and it exists for no good reason, as we have plenty of evidence to show that adoptee rights bills work for the benefit of the greatest number of people.

I do not know whether these essays I write are making a difference or not, but I feel compelled to share my experience. If I don't, who will? As an older adopted person, it's probably too late for me to learn much more about my personal history, but it's not too late for many others. I write in the hopes that my voice, along with so many others, can play some small part in advancing the cause of adoptee rights, so that other human beings affected by the sealed records era won't be made to feel guilty just for attempting to discover the truth about their own lives.

On Being Generic Ethnic

By Lynn Grubb

Last week when I was at work, a Hispanic gentleman came into my place of business. He asked me in Spanish if I spoke Spanish, and I responded, "Un poco," meaning, "A little." He then asked me if I was Hispanic. I replied, "That is an unsolved mystery."

This scenario repeats frequently. People want to know my background. For some reason, they ask me all the time. A friend once said I looked "generic ethnic," meaning I could pass for many different backgrounds. I could be Greek, Italian, Spanish— the list goes on. I find it to be one of many cruel twists of fate in my closed adoption.

I feel bad for those innocent, inquiring people. They don't know what they're getting into when they ask me, the person who won't lie just to make general conversation easy.

Part of the lottery of closed adoption is you may, if you're lucky, get factual information about your ethnicity from an adoption agency (assuming you even had an agency to begin with), or if you are unlucky (like me), you may not. And even in this wonderful internet age, adopted people can't just log on to Ancestry.com to access this. You need a name to begin with.

I received my non-identifying adoption information when I was in my 20s. Make no mistake, I use the word "information" loosely as it was very brief and left much to the imagination. I had identified with being Italian for most of my life. I needed to know what my ethnicity was from a young age, so in order to satisfy that need, I chose to believe what other people said about how I looked, and later, I chose to believe what my adoption paperwork said. My parents had no information to offer me and I didn't identify with their family background. Inside, I knew mine was different because I looked different from them.

Looking back, it's very sad to me that instead of knowing and being told like most children know or are told, I listened to what others told me I was. They seemed to know who I was more than I knew myself. I believe this scenario can play out in many ways in the lives of adoptees, from ethnicity to career choice. It's a way we give away power: "I don't know who I am or where I come from, so I have to listen to others."

In no way was this my adoptive parents' fault. They were set up to fail in trying to satisfy their child's curiosity and valid need to know. I had a vehement argument with my second-grade teacher that I did not come from a woman's tummy; I came from a Cradle, the name of my adoption agency. My mother went in to defend me, as it was clear my teacher didn't understand my situation; my mother had given background info to my teacher, but she failed to read it. Misunderstandings like this one are common in adoption.

As an adult, when my need to know and understand who I was became more pronounced, I truly had no options for getting answers, as my original mother had made no contact with the agency since my relinquishment. I had no way of contacting her to ask questions. I was unaware of her identity due to Illinois' closed records and sealed birth certificates. My only other option was to sign up for a "matching" registry in my state of birth, which was useless considering nobody had ever heard of it, least of all my non-computer-savvy original mother. I signed up anyway and waited.

Fast forward to 2006. I am 40 years old. And my original mother, during one of our first phone calls, informs me that she never gave any "information" about my father to the agency. I have often wondered what was going through the minds of the social workers in 1966 when they were deciding what to write down in my records. Maybe the conversation went like this:

This one's mother won't say who the father is. We can't just say there is no information about the father. That won't look good to a prospective adoptive couple. OK, let's make him a few years older than her. We'll go with Italian since the baby has black hair and light skin. We'll make him educated. We don't want anything to discourage someone from adopting.

While I acknowledge the intent may have been for my benefit (which is a real stretch for me), the impact on my psychological well-being was damaging. Not to mention the fact that lying on legal documents is unethical. I would have had more respect for the agency if their social workers had just written "unknown." The hard truth is better than lies—even when you believe you are protecting somebody.

My husband recently compared this thinking to what happened in the 1950s when "I Love Lucy" was a hit. Lucy became pregnant by her husband and co-star, Desi Arnaz. The producers and censors of the show were very worried that the American public would have a problem with the pregnancy. Lucy and Desi were never shown sleeping in the same bed. CBS wouldn't allow the word "pregnant" to be used, so they settled on "expecting." This reminded my husband of closed adoption. Closed adoption was, in part, a result of this same prudish, care-what-everyone-else-thinks mindset.

I am adopted for one reason, because "unmarried women didn't raise their children back then," as said by my original mother.

Unmarried women were treated with contempt for doing what nature intended (see *The Girls Who Went Away* by Ann Fessler). If you were unmarried and pregnant, you weren't valued. "Baby daddy" was valued even less.

I highly doubt my adoptive parents cared one way or another about my ethnicity. They were just thrilled to have me. They were never told my ethnicity. They were told nothing about me. The adoption agency social workers made decisions that put me into not only ethnic purgatory, but also medical purgatory for most of my life.

My original mother was born with a rare condition, a hole in her heart that required emergency surgery. Somehow this information never made it into my file. In fact, the agency's idea of health history was, "Everybody was in good health." No follow-ups. Did someone get diabetes later? Or cancer? Apparently it didn't matter to my adoption agency, as I was long gone and forgotten.

This agency is more progressive than some. They offer post-adoption services. I hired them to find my original mother. However, they only help you if you ask—and pay, a lot! There is no proactive contact to update you on medical conditions or to let you know a parent is looking for you. If you don't ask, you don't receive. And even if you ask, you will get only what the state deems you worthy of receiving due to adoption files being sealed by the Court .

Illinois has recently opened birth certificates to those adoptees whose original mothers didn't sign a contact veto. What they don't tell you is that most of our fathers aren't on those birth certificates anyway.

How does one undo an identity built on lies? How does one emotionally disconnect from an identity that was constructed over a long period of time, especially when there isn't accurate information to replace it with?

How does one become un-Italian?

My son's maturing into a young man has brought many questions from high school friends about whether he is Hispanic or Asian. His black hair runs on both sides of the family (mostly Indian/English/German/Irish), but unfortunately for him, he inherited my generic ethnic look. He really wants to know about the missing side of his DNA. I wish I had an answer for him. My son's latest coping mechanism, which he finds funny, is to tell everyone he is Cuban, because he says "being Cuban is cool."

People generally don't expect to hear, or want to hear for that matter, that you have no freakin' clue who your father is. This experience of not knowing your father is both painful and unusual in our society. It is usually associated with negative stereotypes such as bastards and mistakes. You hear about "those people" but you don't expect to be talking to one in the flesh. The reality is that most people know who their fathers are. And if they weren't adopted and have questions about their fathers, they can look on their birth certificates or ask relatives for that information. My husband's father and stepfather both physically left the family during his childhood; however, he knew where they were.

And most importantly, he knew who they were.

Not true for adoptees in closed adoption. We have no such stories of our original parents. Our histories are like black holes.

Ask an Adoptee: Semantics

By Christina Worthington

The question being posed to us was as follows:

"I would like to know if those of you that have been reunited with your mother, realize that you were not 'given away.' I keep seeing that in most of your blogs and it must have been a terrible thing to have inside one's head, especially a child's head.

"Most of the mothers of loss that I know, including myself, did not EVER give you away. Most of us were coerced and had absolutely NO choice in the matter. Most of us had our babies 'taken away,' never did we 'give them away.' I would love to say to the children in you all, NO, your mother did not give you away. Be interested in hearing your comments."

A lot. Several. Most. I have come to hate these words.

"A lot of adoptees I know grew up happy and well-adjusted."

"Several adoptive parents adopted because they wanted to save an orphan."

"Most natural mothers did not give their children away."

My own mother and I have a very special bond. After our first contact, we clicked instantly. Bonded immediately. But she did give me away 37 years ago. I was left at the hospital as she walked out and I was not adopted until six days later.

I was given up. Abandoned. Adopted.

Honestly, the language doesn't matter. It all boils down to a mother and child being separated. Embrace your story. It's yours. But please don't take away mine.

I'm not sure my adoptive parents ever actually said, "You were given up." They just told me that they wanted another daughter and the agency called them. The whole "given up" conversation never came up and wasn't something that was ever explicitly said to me. But it's how I felt. Then and now.

I deserve to live my truth.

Adoption Culture Clash

By Julie Stromberg

When adoptees talk to each other, the topic of culture clashes we might experience often comes up. The most obvious and socially accepted take on this concept might come from an adoptee who was removed from her original culture through adoption and raised in another—an ethnic culture clash. Or perhaps, an adoptee who was born into a family with modest means and raised in another that had more from a monetary standpoint—a socioeconomic culture clash.

I cannot write from either of those vantage points. I'm an adoptee who was born of one Catholic, white, middle-class, New England family and raised in another Catholic, white, middle-class, New England family. My adoption was most definitely a lateral move. And seeing as how Catholic Charities placed me with people who lived only eight miles from my natural families, I hardly had to forfeit my regional culture. So, on paper it seems as though this particular topic of clashing cultures in adoption doesn't pertain to me.

Thanks to my fellow Lost Daughter, Rebecca Hawkes, I have come to realize that all adoptees face a culture clash of sorts. Ours is a very adoption-focused society. Please note that I wrote adoption-focused. This is very different from adoptee-focused. Here in the United States, our culture has an overly romanticized and idealistic love affair going on with adoption that brings to mind unicorns, rainbows and puffy hearts. Some days it seems as if everyone is prancing around in

Adoptionland, where the clouds are made of spun sugar and the roads are lined with red licorice. Nothing bad ever happens in Adoptionland, and all of the adopted children feel nothing but gratitude for being placed in this world where they make the dreams of adults come true. Because here in Adoptionland, the focus is on the people who want children instead of on the children themselves. How wonderful! Or maybe not so much.

For many of us adoptees, adoption is an extremely complicated experience rife with confusion and mystery, mainly because the adoption industry doesn't respect us or serve our needs. Seriously, if you see a bunch of adult adoptees floating down the fruit punch river in a candy cane canoe waving their original birth certificates and flags representing their ethnic backgrounds, let me know.

There are people out there in Adoptionland who actually fight against the restoration of an adoptee's right to obtain her own, factual birth certificate. There are adoptive parents out there in Adoptionland who relegate the original mother of the child they are privileged to be raising to the role of "birth person." There are adoption agencies out there in Adoptionland that charge higher fees for white newborns and lower fees for black infants. There are state governments out there in Adoptionland making sure that so-called open adoption agreements are not enforceable. And all of this is totally acceptable within our adoption-focused culture!

As an adult adoptee, I do not fit in here in Adoptionland. Never did. Never will. I was taken from my home turf of Bioland, where I would actually know from whom and from where I came, and forced to live in Adoptionland, where I was handed a fake birth certificate that people tell me I should feel grateful about. Talk about a culture clash.

I Am An Angry Adoptee

By Karen Pickell

Go ahead. Call me angry because I am.

I'm not mad at my adoptive parents, though. They came of age in a social climate that was much different than our current one. My mom and dad were both born in the 1930s. As children, they lived through the worst depression this country has ever seen. They grew up during World War II; Pearl Harbor was their 9/11.

When my mom was a young woman, she had "female problems" (that was the terminology) which led to a hysterectomy. I can't help but sympathize with her desire to adopt in order to experience motherhood for herself. I'm awed that my dad was so devoted to her that he agreed to give up the dream of having his own biological children in order to be with her.

It would be a mistake for me to judge them based on the information we have available to us today about how adoption really works. My parents lived in the same Midwestern city their entire lives. In fact, my mom still lives in the neighborhood where she grew up (my dad passed away in 2003). I was raised in that same neighborhood. I attended the same grade school and high school she did. Neither of my parents attended college; they were traditional, working class people who were thrilled to be able to own their own home and one car. The entirety of their lives existed in that neighborhood. They got all their news from the console television in our living room and from the morning newspaper delivered to the milk chute beside our back door.

When my parents decided to adopt, they turned to the Catholic Church for guidance and assistance, because their faith was the driving force in their lives. Their parish pastor was the final word on how they were to conduct themselves in all situations. I became their daughter via Catholic Charities in Cleveland, Ohio, back in 1968. At that time, there was no post-adoption support offered. My parents weren't informed that their adopted child might be in distress as a result of being separated from the woman who gave birth to her. They were told the bare minimum about my birth parents; all they knew was that my "real" parents (the terminology used when I was growing up) were teenagers, so obviously they couldn't take care of a baby. I'm sure Catholic Charities expressed what a wonderful, charitable thing my parents were doing by adopting me and assured them that I would blend right into their family since my ancestry was similar to theirs. I was a good match for them.

If I'm starting to sound sarcastic, remember, I said I was angry.

I'm not angry at my adoptive parents, though. And I'm not mad at my birth parents, either. They were teenagers when I was born, just as Catholic Charities said. My mother was the second of four children in a Catholic family that lived in a very modest area on the west side of Cleveland, seventy blocks or so closer to downtown than the neighborhood where I grew up with my adoptive parents. My mother attended the local public high school.

My father began attending the same high school when he moved into the Catholic boys' home that was located very near my mother's house. Both of his parents had died, and none of his parents' relatives was able to raise him and his five siblings; they were scattered, with the eldest sent to the orphanage and the youngest placed in foster care until they could be adopted.

By the time my mother and grandmother went to Catholic Charities for help, my mother was halfway through her pregnancy, and by her account, my grandfather was pissed. He wouldn't even consider letting her keep her baby. My grandmother's sister offered to take me, but he wouldn't hear of that either because he didn't want anyone to know that his 15-year-old daughter had gotten herself in trouble.

Look at my grandfather if you want to understand the beginning of my anger.

The non-identifying information I received from Catholic Charities when I began the search for my birth mother talks about a pregnancy "characterized by fear." It states that my mother was intimidated by her father, that he was "openly hostile and unrelenting," that my grandmother was verbally and physically abused by him when she tried to advocate for my mother.

My own grandfather, a man whose blood I share, was the primary reason I sit here today writing this essay. If he had shown compassion for his daughter when she became pregnant, I might never have been separated from my mother. It seems so simple, but I know it wasn't. He died before I found my mother, so I never had the opportunity to face him myself and ask why he did it, why he banished me–his first grandchild–from his family. I can only guess his motivations, and based on the little I know about him, my best guess is that his reaction was a mixture of rejection of the financial burden of having to care for me combined with an intense sense of shame over the fact that my mother, his daughter, committed the sin of having sex outside of marriage. Maybe he felt he would be seen as a bad father because he hadn't been able to control his daughter's behavior. Maybe he thought he would be ostracized by his family or his community. Maybe I should have compassion for him, but I don't. He hurt my grandmother, he hurt my mother, and he hurt me. Shame on him.

I am very angry at my grandfather, but that is only the beginning of my anger. I understand that, like my adoptive parents, he grew up in a different society than the one I live in now. My grandfather, the man who kicked me out of his house before I took my first gasp of air, was only four years older than my adoptive father. I imagine they shared many of the same values.

For old-time Catholics, the laws of the Church took precedence over the laws of any secular government. Catholic teaching dictated that the manner in which I was conceived made me illegitimate, a bona fide bastard. I was legitimized, though, when I was adopted by a married, Catholic couple, and my birth and baptismal certificates were altered to list me as their daughter. This was the right way for things to be done.

Before I met my birth mother, I read in the report of my non-identifying information from Catholic Charities that my grandfather was abusive toward both her and my grandmother while I was in utero. I suspect he was abusive long before then as well. When my mother and grandmother went to Catholic Charities for help, did they receive shelter from this abusive man? Did they receive counseling to help them find a way to build a life for themselves beyond his control? There is no indication in the report that they were offered assistance of any kind. It does say, though, that my mother was unable to room at a local maternity home because her family couldn't afford it. Now maybe you see how deep my anger goes. Where was the charity from Catholic Charities? I've sat at Masses listening to pleas from the pulpit for funds to cover beautiful stained glass windows or to build new recreation facilities. I watched my adoptive parents every week drop an envelope into a wicker basket out of duty to the Church. I imagine my birth grandparents likely did the same. Yet there was no money to pay for my mother's bed at the maternity home. And after all her years of praying, there was no support for my birth grandmother either to escape her abusive husband or to help her daughter keep her baby.

I suppose it's naïve for me to expect Catholic Charities to advise a woman on how to leave her husband, when the Catholic Church expressly prohibits divorce and actively encourages making marriage work at any cost. It's ridiculous to criticize them for contributing to the overwhelming sense of shame that continues to oppress my mother when the Catholic Church has made it very clear that sex outside of marriage is just plain wrong. The Church has never wavered on this teaching.

I am angry at the Catholic Church for its role in separating me from my family. I am angry that the Church accepts no responsibility for the pain it has caused. I am outraged that anyone ever thought, or that they think now, that it's okay to rip families apart in the name of God. To the Catholic Church, I say, how dare you brainwash my grandfather into rejecting his own grandchild, how dare you shame my mother into hating a part of herself that was perfectly normal and natural, and how dare you label me or any other child as illegitimate. Is any of this what Jesus would do? I think not.

When I think about why I was separated from my birth mother, why I was sent to live with strangers, I think about how it could have, and should have, been different. My mother should have been supported rather than shamed and ostracized. Her family and community should have rallied to help her raise her child—me. She did not have to suffer the loss of her firstborn child. I did not have to suffer the loss of my mother. I did not need to be adopted.

Yes, I am an angry adoptee for good reason.

What's in a Name?

By Elle

When my adoptive parents decided to christen me with a Swedish name, they decided to keep my original name as a middle name—a link to my heritage and past perhaps. At least this is a nice thought. My mum once explained this to me, but I can't recall us ever discussing my name.

I have always felt like the name they gave me didn't really suit me, but I can't deny that having a Swedish name helped me avoid being confronted with racism at times.

Once I had met my Korean birth family for the first time, I finally knew what name I would pick for myself. I took back my Korean name with some minor alterations. The only name I kept was my adoptive parents' surname because it was a name that runs in the family. I thought that even though I would be changing my personal name by reclaiming my Korean name, keeping a family name from my adoptive family sounded like a nice compromise. I managed to honor my Korean birth family and my Swedish adoptive family at the same time.

I should have prepared myself for a big reaction from my adoptive family. Maybe they thought a name change was just an idea that would pass, but the subject always managed to return to my mind. Once I received the official grant of a personal name change, it meant my name was validated by Swedish law. Thus, my new name became a part of me. Neither of my two families reacted positively, not even my Korean birth family.

Today I understand why my birth family reacted in such a strange way. My birth family was proud of me and of the fact that they could say they had a relative in Europe. I think they even bragged about me to show off in some way. When I changed my Swedish name legally, it meant the link to Sweden would become less apparent. Maybe my siblings thought I would try to claim a place in my birth family. It is true that I did want a place in my birth family, but only with the intention of receiving the love I always craved and missed during my childhood.

I see my birth name as the only thing that came with me from Korea to Sweden—the only thing that nobody else could take away. I feel like my name is something I am entitled to decide for myself.

Would the reaction I received from my parents and my birth family have been any different if I had decided to change my surname legally instead of my personal name?

I think changing my surname might have been easier for my Swedish parents to accept. On the other hand, I do believe my birth family would have felt much more threatened by the thought of me changing my surname because that instantly leads to inheritance. Of course, I have no interest in any inheritance from my birth family. According to the law, I legally have no right to claim any inheritance from my Korean parents or siblings. I know this, but I doubt my siblings do.

At this point, I suspect that my families believe I will eventually reverse the name change. But to me, my new, real name signifies so much. It is a part of my identity. Yet even with this new name, I feel I will go through life with constant feelings of confusion and longing—a longing for a life that never will be.

My Adoptee Family Tree is Actually an Orchard

By Laura Dennis

When my fifth-grade teacher assigned a family tree project, I did mine using my parents' families, as in my adoptive heritage (sounds like an oxymoron). Dad in particular took the activity very seriously, calling his mother for correct name spellings going five generations back.

No big deal, it was just a family tree. And yet, even at age 10, something about the whole activity felt strange. Only I didn't have the words to explain what that weird feeling was about.

No one thought to incorporate my true-and-very-real biological branch, which was odd because family trees track bloodlines. Even though my adoption was closed, we had a letter, which I cherished, from the private adoption agency. The letter had no identifying information, of course, but it included the age, height, and weight of my first mom's siblings and her parents, along with a few details about my biological great-grandparents. We could have somehow integrated those tidbits into the project. I know we didn't have names, but we had birth years and genders and something is better than nothing, right?

For over a decade now, I have had a lovely reunion with my first mother. It's great that my two (non-adopted) kids have both my adoptive mom and my first mom as grandmas—more love to go around and all that. Nevertheless, the blighted branch that is my generation will continue to hang over my children and so on down the line. I'm left wondering who will go and who will get to stay on the family tree.

What about my biological father's side? I'm not even in contact with the man; he truly wants nothing to do with me. He doesn't even consider his three other children to be related to me.

"They're my half-brothers and sisters," I once explained.

"I never thought about it that way," he responded. Baffling.

I've decided that while there are some missing limbs, my family tree isn't broken; it's just got a helluva lot of branches. It's also more than one tree—an orchard, really, with some trees close and others way off in the distance. Even those diseased branches, with love and care and open-mindedness, have the potential to grow beautifully.

Today there are so many ways to create a family. My 4-year-old daughter has a friend with two moms. She says, "Just like you, Mommy!" Not exactly. Her friend's mommies are married to each other. No matter. My daughter will understand everything eventually, and I have no intention of hiding the messiness. Families have step-, biological, adopted and foster children. Family life is messy. Heck, life is messy. Perhaps if we acknowledge this reality, we can embrace reunions and accept families whose structure is different than our own, even if it means drawing entire orchards.

Half Blank

By Carlynne Hershberger

My husband and I were talking and daydreaming the other day about a trip we'd like to take. He's been to Europe, but I have not. I'd like for him to show me the sights. We could do the tourist thing—see castles, explore the countryside, or take a river cruise. It's not something we can do anytime soon. But in the spirit of our daydream, I thought I'd look into the requirements for a passport. I had never needed one before so I never thought about it. The first thing I noticed was the requirement for the original birth certificate (OBC) and that the date on the certificate had to be within one year of the date of birth.

Well, my birth certificate is amended and is dated several years after my birth because I was adopted by my dad. He's the only dad I've ever known, but he's not my natural father. I guess this makes me an adoptee-lite along with being a natural mother. I haven't talked about this other connection I have with adoption before because of the conditioning I grew up with. I didn't even find out about my adoption until I was 26. Here I am now at 52 years old just starting to talk about it. My family felt there was such a stigma connected to adoption that they didn't want anyone to know— not even me, the one most affected.

Since becoming involved with the adoption community, I've read stories from adoptees about finding out the truth as an adult. I can relate. Although I was raised by my mother and knew her side of the family, there was still another entire family I know very little about. To find out that you are not who you think you are is mind blowing. It's like your world tilts on its axis and nothing is the same again. One of the first thoughts I had was *Wow, I'm not really Cuban?*

Even the simple act of looking in the mirror changes. I didn't think any differently about my dad and I don't love him any less. It just brought another whole element into the equation about my identity. When I think about how much the news affected me, I can really feel for the adoptees who find this out when they're older and have zero information about either side of their natural families.

I found out about my own adoption six years after losing my daughter and when my third child was just under a year old. I was trying to raise two little ones and keep myself together while dealing with the loss of my baby girl. There was a lot going on, to say the least. So, I stewed on it for a while, but then put it away. I had to focus on my kids. Now that I've started blogging, talking to other people in the adoption constellation, and writing letters and comments to people about access to OBCs for adoptees, all of this stuff about my own adoption comes rushing back to the forefront. I don't know what that means for me. I'd like to find out more about my natural father's family. Maybe it'll mean no passport for me. I haven't researched enough yet to know.

It seems like it doesn't matter what angle you're coming from. There's shame and secrecy involved.

No more lies, no more shame, no more hiding. I'm done with that already.

Images of Waiting Children

By Liberty Ferda

We love the Dave Thomas Foundation for Adoption. They do a lot of great work encouraging people to adopt kids from foster care. Among the most notable achievements are the federal tax breaks Dave successfully advocated for in the '90s and, of course, his Wendy's fast food restaurant's practice of donating a percentage of its profits toward adoption.

I remember growing up thinking that Wendy's was special because Wendy was adopted, which I viewed as positive. I didn't realize that Dave was the adopted one and the daughter he named the restaurant after was his biological child, probably because I wanted so badly to know another adopted daughter and, therefore, chose to believe Wendy was a fellow adoptee. She also had crazy hair like me.

These days I don't spend time gazing out the window of my parents' car looking for Wendy's restaurants. But I do get emails from the Dave Thomas Foundation. I appreciate all the work it does, but I have to say that sometimes I feel uneasy about the images of waiting children the foundation uses in promotions.

Maybe it's because the images could play into that old "rescue the child" attitude. The pictured kids are often alone, gazing upward, as if waiting to be picked up. You want to reach into the posters and hold the kids. Which is the point.

46

Yet there's more to it. Yes, you are helping a child when you foster or adopt, but if you start with a "missionary" mindset and expect the child to be ever grateful and good because you saved them from certain squalor, the child is probably going to experience feelings of anger and resentment at some point. It's demoralizing to be thought of as a charity case.

Images, in advertising especially, tend not to invite complexity. They activate viewers' emotions much faster than words do. This probably has something to do with the right-brain/left-brain thing that a linguist or psychologist would know more about than me. What bothers me is that the emotion these images evoke is a troubling one: Pity.

Don't simply pity the poor orphan. If you seek to foster or adopt, pity will make the task before you seem too easy. From what I've seen, that attitude reduces the situation and can lead prospective adoptive/foster parents to hold unrealistic expectations. Pity does not invite conversation or engagement—it's a one-way emotion. No one wants to be pitied or be made to feel that she is getting a handout. At the same time, pity seems to set up an expectation on the part of the "giver" that the "receiver" be grateful, only grateful. With that expectation, the "giver" will be disappointed, even alarmed, by complicated emotions that very well might be expressed by the adopted/fostered person alongside gratefulness—anger, confusion, fear, isolation, the list goes on. Respect the child as a full person who probably won't think of you as a savior, and be OK with that. Do step into adoption or foster care, but do it with recognition of the child's hurts and struggles, and have an openness to learn from the child. Adoption isn't a rescue mission—it's a paradox of torn flowers.

Adoptee Lineage: Hands Off My Ancestors

By Michelle Lahti

Come in. Have a seat here at the counter. I'll put on a fresh pot of coffee. Just a sec, I need to grab one of my photo albums. I want to show you a picture.

Ah, here it is: The year is 1974. A little girl wears a paper-bag vest and a headdress decorated with construction paper feathers. She holds the hand of her teacher, who is dressed in a long black skirt and black blouse, with an apron, collar, and hat all in white. Like other kindergarteners across the country, the little girl is learning about the pilgrims, the first Thanksgiving, and the Mayflower.

She has no idea that she's learning about her very own ancestors.

Because of the laws of her state, she has no way of knowing that she is a direct descendant of not only one or two, but of several passengers who crossed the Atlantic Ocean in 1620 on that famous ship. She has no way of knowing that the feast her class is celebrating is not just her nation's history, but family history.

The little girl smiles at us from across the years, full of sweetness and innocence. She is excited to be wearing her costume even though the paper bag is stiff and makes an unpleasant sound. She is loved; her life is good. She does not yet realize that her nation, which deems its beginnings of such importance that it requires school children from one coast to the other learn about them, does not deem her worthy to know her own origins or ancestry. She does not yet know of the pain that will later come as a result of being forced by law to live in this contextual vacuum.

You may wonder why the little girl is denied the right to have information about herself and her heritage. The answer is simple.

She is adopted.

The little girl grows. As a young woman, she attends a college rich in Dutch heritage. She occasionally feels out of place when she hears, "If you're not Dutch, you're not much," even though it's said in good-natured fun. In actuality, she does have Dutch ancestry, and will later be able to trace her lineage directly to people living in the Netherlands as far back as the ninth century.

She, however, has no legal right to know this.

She is adopted.

She marries and has children. She home-schools. She and her children study American history, and with it, learn about the Mayflower Compact. She reads parts of the document aloud to her children. If she knew, she would tell them that this significant bit of history was written by her (and their) many-times-great-grandfathers. She takes her children to Jamestown Settlement. If she knew, she would tell them of the great-and-then-some-grandfather who spent time there before later voyaging back to Plymouth on the Mayflower. But these stories are not known to her. Her basic human right to know her own origins, and thus to trace her own ancestry, is not legally upheld. Her original birth certificate was locked away—sealed—when her adoption was finalized, and she is not allowed to obtain it.

This is, of course, my story. Both the faded picture and the rich heritage are mine. While the picture warms my heart with its familiarity, my family tree, only recently known to me, is like a shiny, new treasure. Every glimpse thrills me. Those of my ancestors who are historically famous engage my imagination and cause my heart to flutter; those for whom I know nothing more than names, I equally value simply because they are mine.

Not everyone, though, believes that I should have the right to know my own heritage, or that my ancestry should be valued or honored.

I am adopted.

While I somehow avoided the typical family tree project in my school years, I was surprised by the intensity of my reaction when my oldest son was given the assignment in his social studies class. The students were to trace their lineage as far back as possible, on both their father's and mother's sides, paying particular attention to any immigrant or Native American ancestors. A knot formed in my stomach. How could my son complete the assignment accurately when he could only trace my side back to, well, me?

At his parent-teacher conference, I gathered my courage and blurted out my concern. "We know my son's heritage on his dad's side, but he won't have anything for mine because I was adopted."

The young teacher blinked. He shifted uncomfortably in his chair as though I'd broken some unwritten rule. "Um ... just have him use your adopted family." Blink.

Right. Of course. Just use my adoptive family.

Except this assignment wasn't about relationships or love or shared memories or emotional ties. It was about tracing one's lineage, about creating an opportunity for the students to explore the means through which they ended up citizens of this nation. While I harbor no ill will toward my adoptive parents' ancestors, their journeys brought neither me nor my son to this place.

Eventually, my son completed the assignment using my adoptive family. It felt like a giant lie.

The project was likely more painful for me than it was for my son. I'm glad it wasn't something asked of me in my younger years, yet it's a task frequently endured by young adoptees. Such assignments have often been the topic of conversation among fellow adoptive families. Many parents offer advice-filled compassion and wisdom, and share ways that adopted youth can structure family trees to reflect their situation more authentically and to honor all who belong to them.

Other adoptive parents, however, respond with shockingly little empathy for the adoptee experience or acknowledgement of the adoptee's factual genealogy:

"My kids have a woman who birthed them. They've all done autobiographies without any issue. I guess if it was an open adoption, then there would be a difference. I would feel terrible for my students that are in foster care. Now that would be bad."

"Biology is not what makes a family. A family tree comes from family. My adopted daughter has one family, ours. She has biological parents whom she most likely will never meet. They are not a family until there is relationship."

"I don't see my daughter as having more than one family just because she is adopted. We are her family."

"In this day and age, if you can be whatever sex you want to be, then you can define family any way you want."

"I'm his mother and I have the birth certificate to prove it!"

"You know, my truth isn't your truth, isn't her truth. ... Family is what you make it. That's my truth."

"We just fill it out for our family. Why would I include anything else? Tell [your adopted child] this is your family!"

Suffice it to say, I disagree with the above remarks entirely. Such insensitive comments, which I've seen online and heard in face to face conversations, have made me ache for young adoptees who may not yet be able to advocate for themselves. A recent dialogue in an online adoption group even gave me my first and only case of emotionally-triggered hives, as many adoptive parents there refused to see the factual ancestry of adopted persons as being of value or worthy of acknowledgement.

While terminology and the definition of family may be debatable, the fact that adoptees (aside from those in kinship adoption) have genetic ancestry different from that of their adoptive parents is undisputable. Adoption neither negates nor creates biological relatedness. Those who argue adamantly about the definition of "family," insisting that the adoptive family is the only family to the extent of dismissing the adoptee's factual lineage, miss the point that an adopted person's acceptance of this attitude forces her to deny significant parts of herself.

Adoption may legally sever filiation, but it does not make members of the family of origin cease to exist. Regardless of the circumstances surrounding the separation from our first families, regardless of whether we have identifying information about our first families, the truth is that adopted individuals came from real, actual people, who came from real, actual people, who came from real, actual people, ad infinitum.

Living without knowledge of one's own origin is not for the faint of heart. During the years of knowing next to nothing about the people I came from (all but one year of my life at this writing), I felt a deep loneliness. Without knowledge of my origins, I lacked a connection to the world. I was an entity unto myself.

Today, I know who I am. Now that I'm no longer prevented from having critical pieces of self-knowledge and connection with my original family, I am experiencing life with new peace, empowerment, and freedom.

Adoptees deserve the dignity of having our biological origins acknowledged, both by those who raise us and by society at large, and of having such information made available to us by law. We should have the right to represent all who belong to us on school-project family trees if we so choose. We are human beings with human ancestry, undeserving of archaic laws which keep us from obtaining documents pertaining to our own histories, such as our own, original birth certificates, which other citizens acquire with ease. No person should have her familial history annihilated simply because care outside of the biological family may have been necessary. No person should be denied such significant self-knowledge simply because of adoption.

Come in. Have a seat on the couch. I've finished the coffee, but I'll start a new pot. We're studying medieval history this year, and there's a book I'd like to show you. We're just about to discuss one of my many-times-great-grandfathers. You might have heard of him.

His name was Charlemagne.

Race Matters More for a Middle Schooler

By Rosita Gonzalez

The bell at my son's middle school will ring this coming week. He's tentative, and I'm bracing myself. Last fall, one of our mother-son breakfasts began like this.

"Mom, someone at school told me no one would date me because I'm mixed race."

My heart sank, but I hid my hurt. I said, "Did you tell him, 'That's okay, because I won't date racist people'?"

"No! I never thought of that," he replied excitedly. "That's good."

I explained I had many years of experience thinking of comebacks. Yet, this wasn't the first time my son had experienced prejudice. He had his first bout with it when he was eight. At the time, he didn't seem fazed, but he admitted then that he had held onto that memory as well.

As we talked further, he felt better. He realized that he was not alone, that his mother had grown up with the same, and that, as author Eric Hoffer once said, "Rudeness is the weak man's imitation of strength."

I've spoken about some personal incidents of racism in my blog, but recently, I've been able to pinpoint some things for myself.

From the 1970s to the 1990s, my life was about assimilation. I wanted to be white. I wanted to blend into the Appalachian human fabric and disappear. During those years in the South, those around me often reminded me that I was different, strange, or simply "not normal."

My mother tried to console me when these cruelties happened, but over time, I realized that she truly did not know how I felt. My father, on the other hand, did to some degree. As a Puerto Rican whose English was heavily accented, he had endured his share of racism. We spoke some about it, but rarely.

I have spent my life longing to fit in racially. In Virginia, I found my two closest friends, Katherine and Adrienne, who are strong Asian women. I have blogged about how they taught me a great deal about Asian culture, another crucial step in my development.

Together, we work to help our children assimilate in a country that values whiteness while devaluing and mocking people of color. When I married, I believed that our children would fare better than I had with a father who was white. As my son becomes more self-aware, though, what I am realizing is my own naiveté.

I thought I could learn from my life and spare him and his sister the ridicule. My husband and I bought our house based on the public schools that had more racial diversity. We avoided the rural South. We talk openly about race as a family. Despite all these efforts, I know that my children will face not only the racial ridicule, but also a life of racial ambivalence.

This torments me. It also fuels my ambition to see change. Children of transracial adoptees inherit their parents' racial ambivalence. They are the second generation, and they need to be recognized as much as, if not more than, the adoptees.

Reunion & Family

You Only Have One Mother!

By Liberty Ferda

I'm writing this from Abraham Lincoln Memorial Hospital in Springfield, Ill., where Mom is recovering from post-radiation surgery to remove cancerous tumors. Thankfully, the director of the writing center was very understanding about my leaving my teaching duties mid-week even though the semester just started. As I spoke with her on the phone, trying to figure out how I could rearrange appointments and/or get someone to cover for me, she said, "Go. Just go."

Her next words threw me for a loop: "You only have one mother! Right?"

Um, well, not exactly.

"Y-yes," I said, to keep things simple and move the conversation along. Her question kept creeping into my thoughts during the nine-hour drive to Illinois. I have two mothers—my birth mother, who gave me life and relinquished me into foster care/adoption, and my adoptive mom, who raised me. I wondered whether my birth mother has ever had major surgery, and I was sad that I didn't even know the answer. I wondered whether I would jump in my car and drive nine hours if my birth mom were having surgery. I think I probably would if I knew she wanted me there, but sadly, it would take more consideration. I'm just not as close to her, and sometimes I feel that our relationship is strained. I always try to recognize and validate her role in my life, but truthfully, I am much closer to my adoptive mom. We've had many more years to work on getting along and growing a

59

lasting connection.

I wish it didn't have to be this way. I think the relationship is difficult for my birth mother. How could it not be? At its root is heartbreak, loss—a relationship established and terminated almost immediately post-birth, then restarted 25 years later. This is the nature of adoption.

As I watch Mom's painful recovery from a surgery not unlike a Cesarean birth, I think of the pain my birth mother must have experienced when she gave me up. Someday my birth mother and I may be closer, I hope. I have always thought of her and loved her from afar, and she has said it was the same for her. Perhaps all that thinking and loving someone absent can make it hard to bring a relationship to the "reality" realm, the in-touch/in-person world. It may take a few more years before both of us are ready to drop everything and meet the other in the hospital.

So, the answer is "no," a simple "no." I don't only have one mother. My two mothers are different, they have occupied different spaces in my life. But in the end, my love for them is the same.

Reactions to Searching

By Jennifer Anastasi

If you've searched for or are thinking of searching for your natural family, what would you say to those who think your desire to search means you are unhappy in your adoptive family or had a bad childhood? If you don't have a desire to search, what would you say to those who wonder why you have no interest in knowing where you come from?

—Writing prompt at Lost Daughters

I get this one a lot. As a preface, my adoptive family is great. They are not perfect, but I don't know of any parents who are. They made mistakes along the way because they are human. That being said, my parents are amazing. They sacrificed a lot for my sister and me while we were growing up. My dad worked seven days a week. My mom baked cookies, just because. My birthday was treated like a national holiday. We had a vacation home, a family dog, and a wonderful extended family. I have more support than I sometimes know what to do with; I grew up loved and felt it. My parents are proud of the person I have become and they love to brag about my accomplishments. They have stood behind me at every crossroad of my life and have supported me. They haven't always agreed with all my choices, but they have done their best to be there anyway. So, no, my adoptive parents are not bad people, nor did they fail as adoptive parents. Actually, they've done quite the opposite.

My parents raised me to be a strong, independent woman. They used to tell me that I was smart (they still do!). I had potential. I could go to college if I wanted. In fact, they knew I'd get into a good college if I put my mind toward it, and they'd do anything they could to help me. I could be whoever and whatever I wanted to be. I told them I wanted to be a lawyer. My blue-collar parents bit their tongues and told me that was amazing, they were proud of me. I told them I wanted to be a teacher, and they said I'd be great at that because I'm so good with kids. I told them I wanted to do accounting, and they said I was always great with numbers. When I told them accounting wasn't for me and I wanted to be a software engineer, my parents told me I'd be amazing at it because I had a gift when it came to computers.

I remember having trouble with boys. My mom used to pull me into her arms and tell me that someday I'd find a boy who loved me for me. She would tell me never to settle and that I deserved a great man. I needed someone who would respect me and who would push me to be my best self. Until I met that man, I shouldn't settle. I could be independent. I could have my own career. And someday, I could have a family, too. Anything I wanted, I could have, and she'd be there supporting me, no matter what. I was so thankful for her advice when I did meet the right man for me.

I grew up with a strong support system. I believe that people are inherently good. I have compassion for others. All of this, I attribute to my adoptive parents. They raised me right. And because I had received nothing but love and support from them, I had the strength to search. I knew there was a chance—a strong one—that I wouldn't like what I would find. But I searched anyway because I knew my adoptive parents would be there for me if that turned out to be the case. I knew they'd help me pick up the pieces, and I knew they had raised me to be strong enough to do so on my own if I needed to.

My parents didn't fail. In fact, they succeeded. They raised a confident, strong, independent young woman who isn't afraid to tackle life's challenges. It's not always easy. And I make mistakes. I'm far from perfect. However, they did right by me, and I'm proud of the person I am today. I searched because they did their job right. I searched because I had a good childhood. I searched because I had a good childhood. I searched not because I needed to replace the family I already had, but rather because I wanted to find those missing pieces that only my natural family could fill. My adoptive parents gave me the strength to put in the work, and I'll always be glad for that.

Boxes

By Joy Lieberthal Rho

Boxes. I have been thinking a lot about boxes these past few weeks. Boxes to transport my food so I won't lose it with a loss of power. Boxes for toys, diapers and sheets to give to others. Boxes to store my boys' treasures. Boxes (or rather circles) to pick the next president. It's been a busy few weeks.

The box that has been staying with me, though, has been Pandora's. Her box has been quite troublesome lately. It is bittersweet to realize that without the pain, there can be little in the way of true joy, and I struggle to make sense of the idea that oftentimes in adoption, this paradox exists time and time again. Opening the adoption box releases a deposit of ills, loss, grief, black holes, unexplainable emotions, and endless questions. It can open up the inner workings of our mind that remained dormant for decades, open our eyes to an alternate reality that we cannot ever make sense of, and disease our heart with pining. I would love to think that having my birth mother in my life has quelled the pining, but most of the time I am reminded of all I missed, and little of any of the above has been quelled.

Recently, my big boy, P., had a school project that involved putting into a box his short history on this earth, to show his classmates from whence he came. In the creation of this history box, we went through a bunch of pictures and artifacts for his choosing. I had his birth certificate and was acutely aware that mine was missing in the collective.

There are thousands of his baby photos, but none of mine; he had a tangible face to view, something that I have always missed. And yet, I am grateful for what I was able to give him. I loved doing this project with him. He was making his history box, while I was making history for myself along with him.

The history of a child used to be based on a tree concept. A linear concept with roots that an adopted child could not fill and branches that remained nameless. Very frustrating, humiliating and extremely lacking. I am thrilled my son's school is progressive enough to think out of the box instead. P. did a poetic job of choosing photos of his brother, parents, grandparents, great-grandparents, uncles, aunts and cousins, all to be pasted on the outside of his box. The inside he saved for himself—sonogram photo, newborn hat, baby pictures, among other mementos. He surrounded himself with love from family and nestled himself inside. Lovely. I cried. Among the photos were my Umma, my brother, my referral photo, and me in Korea way back when. There was one photo he chose to include that stopped me a bit short. It was of me with my orphanage siblings outside of the orphanage in 1976. I don't know why he chose to include it, but it was amazing to see it there. My history was embedded into his.

While Pandora's box created ills for generations to come, my legacy of loss ends with me. P. honored my past in such a beautiful, subtle way, as one of many components that make him him. The joy of creating my family has given me immeasurable happiness, something I treasure and never take for granted given the empty box I have been holding onto all these years. P. will have his own loss and will grieve aplenty in his soon-to-be-full life. I am glad his grief won't involve loss that undercuts his sense of self, too. P.'s Korean name means "broad foundation." In looking at his box, I am grateful I could be a part of giving him that foundation.

Nature and Nurture

By Julie Stromberg

Adoptees are in the unique position of providing some experiential insight into the topics of nature and nurture. Please note that I wrote "nature and nurture" instead of "nature vs. nurture." This was a deliberate move and one that sets up my thoughts on the matter.

As a mother and an adoptee, it is my feeling that a parent's job is to nurture a child's nature. This goes for both natural and adoptive families. My two sons are born of my husband and me. They are mash-ups of their parents' genetics, yet they are quite different from one another. What works for one in the parenting department might not work for the other. And it is the job of my husband and me to respect who each of our boys is as an individual and to provide the nurturing most appropriate for their innate personalities.

Being our sons' natural parents, my husband and I at least have the genetic recognition that comes with raising children we created ourselves. Our boys each have qualities that we can see in ourselves, and this gives us useful insight regarding how to handle certain situations, because our boys are their natures. That's the essence of who they are. And if we do our best to nurture their natures, they will hopefully enter adulthood with a solid sense of self and identity.

The current adoption system is set up in a way that does not help adoptees understand or connect to our own natures and true selves in any way. It's an identity and sense-of-self guessing game for us. And our adoptive parents are unable to offer the genetic connection we need to develop a comprehensive identity. Our adoptive parents are in the position of having to nurture a nature that is unfamiliar and new. Some adoptive parents are able to recognize this and adjust their parenting approach to meet the unique needs of the adoptee. Others struggle with it and place expectations on the adoptee that go against her essence.

The thing is, our nature is always with us from the moment we are conceived. We come into our adoptive families already programmed by our natural families. And because of this, raising an adopted child is not the same as raising a natural child. Adoptive parents must take a unique approach to parenting in order to nurture a child whose nature did not originate from them. It is my feeling that the most successful of adoptive parents are the ones who find a way to step back and observe the child they are raising so that they can encourage the child's nature to blossom.

It's not a competition. Nurture should not fight with nature in some odd battle of wills to win the ability to offer an adoptee a true sense of self. Our natures simply need to be nurtured in a way that is respectful and understanding of our life circumstances.

Lost—Stranger in the Dark

By Karen Brown Belanger

Last week, I went off on a tangent for hours. I discovered an actress who was the exact right size (my biological mother is only 4' 10" tall, which is a very defining piece of identifying information), had the right hair and eye color, and grew up near where I was relinquished for adoption. After 13 years of serious searching, I had given up and instead put my energy into helping others and adoption reform. Even with the help of the best searchers, it was impossible to make progress with the minor tidbits of information I have and without my biological parents releasing their identities, with no names, cities or states to go on.

However, the searching never goes away and is usually ongoing in some capacity. I will always search faces in crowds. My heart will always skip a beat when I hear, "You look just like someone I know," or when I happen upon a possible match like the one that sparked last week's brief, frantic attempt to "find." Not knowing my biological family has a power over me that will never go away. I cannot "get over it." I cannot leave it in the past. It is my past. I need to move on to the future, though I still feel like a stranger is looking back at me in the mirror.

Stranger in the Dark

Sometimes it seems so close and yet I stand so far away.

I seek the signs along the road to help me find my way.

Long distances I have traveled, yet so many miles to go.

Against all odds, I search around these obstacles that grow.

Traversing unknown territory, I pray someday I'll find.

Solutions to enigmas that will ease my burdened mind.

Like Alice through the looking glass, I strive to comprehend.

These mysteries that unravel in this unfamiliar land.

Clues are few, no indications pointing to an end.

Lost track of all the hours and the time that has been spent.

Revealing truths in this life journey upon which I embark.

To unearth secrets that keep me a stranger in the dark

Mothering While Adopted

By Elaine Penn

Maybe the title to this essay should be "Smothering While Adopted." When I asked my teenage daughter what it's like having an adoptee as a mother, she heartily snorted. As she started laughing, she said, "I know nothing else."

Like a lot of adoptees, my firstborn was the first blood kin I ever laid eyes on. The intensity of being in the presence of someone connected to me on a cellular level was searing. The one thing I knew for sure was that I wouldn't let her slip away—as everyone else had done to me.

Giving birth gave me an overwhelming sensation of finally having someone similar to me. It was intense and over-the-top. Then the in-laws showed up at the hospital. They did what every non-adopted person seems to do when there's a new baby in the family. They immediately started identifying characteristics that belong to the family. They had no idea what comments like "she has long fingers like my side of the family" or "those eyes are mine" did to me. My husband's family are all blood related. They all have similarities. I finally had one person who was blood to me. And it felt like my in-laws came to claim her. It wasn't done on purpose. It was quite normal. Normal, though, isn't something with which an adoptee is familiar.

Finally, when everyone was done "oohing and aahing" and had left my hospital room, a darkness fell over me. I was swirling into overwhelming grief when a wonderful nurse stopped in. She said to me, "Smile." I was emotionally drained and gave her a weak smile. She then said, "Now I see where your baby gets her dimple from." My heart seemed to suspend its beating. I was momentarily breathless. She got something from me. For the first time in my life, someone looked at another human being and commented that she looked like me! Amazing! After all those years of step-siblings joking that I was hatched from an egg pod that came down from another planet and disconnection, I was finally connected to another human being. Thinking about it now, almost 17 years later, that one sentence from that one wonderful nurse instantly brings tears to my eyes.

Two years after my oldest daughter's birth, I had my second daughter. While I was totally astounded again, I think I was too exhausted from having a toddler to revel as much in the gloriousness of connection. This time, I didn't feel the panic that she'd slip away from me and leave me.

Mothering was a foreign concept to me. First, I lost my biological mother through adoption. Then, I lost my adoptive mother through death when I was 4-years-old. I lost my first stepmother through divorce. Thankfully, my second stepmother stuck around, but I was already 17-years-old by the time she entered my life. My second stepmother told me many times that I was a "natural" at being a mother. She told me that my babies responded to me and she could see how much I adored them.

What I never told her was that for the most part, I was filled with sheer panic on the inside.

During their childhood, my kids became involved with adoptee rights because I was involved and they went where I went. People made exceptions for them in archive rooms, research areas, and cemeteries—wherever my searching took me. I can't count the number of people who said, "We usually don't allow children in here." I would reassure them with, "They're my assistants." I had one archivist say that my kids handled the microfiche reels better than most adults. They knew what I needed and could go to the wall of cabinets that held the films and get exactly what I needed. One time, an archivist (who had become accustomed to my assistants and me) brought out the original paperwork I was looking for. It wasn't on a microfiche, but on the original book. It was so brittle that we had to wear gloves to even be near it.

They were involved with every phase of trying to pass a law in New Jersey for adoptee rights. They read and reread my writings. They marched in adoptee rights rallies. They missed school to watch me testify at a hearing. They missed school to watch legislation being voted on. They met a New Jersey Governor and acting Governor. They have been to so many adoptee rights events that people commented how big they were getting and asked them how they were doing in school that year.

Both of my kids have given oral reports to their classes about going to legislative hearings. They brought in their badges (yes, security let them keep them to show off at school). They brought in pictures, stood in front of the class, and taught the class about how a bill becomes (or doesn't become) a law and all the steps that need to be taken. They've been to so many government functions that they're recognized. They even sat through five hours of dry testimony just to be there when I testified.

They saw and felt the emotional toll searching for my birth family and being involved in adoptee rights has taken on me. They were there, and are still there, on the front lines with me.

They have made posters and videos, and participated in a documentary about adoptee rights. They have seen firsthand how a mother's rejection can slice into an adoptee's core. They know that I was a secret and had to sneak around to meet my grandmother. They know that lies have been said about me and they aren't able to defend me. They know, and have seen, the truth and they have seen how that truth gets distorted through media.

They have witnessed me panic and not be able to let go of them. They are letting me know that it's okay to ease up and loosen my grip. They are showing me that I don't have to hold on bear-hug tight all the time. They are teaching me how to be a mother to them. After 17 years, I still don't know how to mother, how to let go, or how to give them enough space to be who they want to be. Why? Because they are the only blood I've ever had.

What's Cooking?

By Von

Standing over a saucepan of sauce for lasagna, concentrating so that it doesn't stick and burn, I thought back over years of cooking and the tips I've learned from dear friends: mustard in the sauce for cauliflower cheese—thank you, Chris; a cupful of water with the butter and flour to start before the milk goes in—thank you, someone now forgotten. So it went on through every step of putting it all together. Food memories, life memories are interwoven through everything that matters.

Many people who cook may have learned from their mothers, fathers or another family member, and it makes me sad to think how hopeless Mum's cooking was. It was inedible and always unappetizing because it was a chore, for which she had no enthusiasm whatsoever. She was creative in other ways, which absorbed her far more than turning out a nice meal. I never felt comfortable with it; what a relief it was to visit the homes of school friends or relatives, where food was wholesome, enjoyed, and celebrated.

I recently spent a relaxing afternoon with a piece of Chick Lit, in which cooking and food feature almost as another character. Italian food and cooking! The aromas, the variety, the richness, and the comfort of it all, so well described you could taste it. I am lucky to have Italian neighbors and to buy most of my vegetables and olive oil from their relatives, who garden professionally a stone's throw away. How I would love to have been brought up in that atmosphere where a love and

76

respect for food runs through everything!

My fellow adoptees can probably guess what's coming next. After reunion with both sides of my family, I discovered all were cooks, some professional, some enthusiastic amateurs. Two of my sisters cooked on an oil rig for riggers and enjoyed themselves immensely. My father cooked for every family celebration until he got too old and infirm to do it—the boy who had starved at the hands of the Christian Brothers and considered himself lucky to get a job in the gardens, so he could surreptitiously eat the produce. He kept poultry and grew vegetables, just as I do, although his ducks were for eating while my geese are for beauty.

The thread that runs through my heritage on both sides is in me and has found its place. This explains one of the reasons why I was the piece of the jigsaw that didn't fit in to the space allotted for me as an adoptee. Part of me came home when I discovered that not just one family, but both had skills, enthusiasm and a love for food and cooking. As Davis Suzuki says, "Our food is our medicine," and my discovery was certainly a big tonic.

Reunion and Open Adoption

By Cathy Heslin

Imagine if you had been able to know your birth parents while you were growing up. Alongside, but not part of your family. Visiting, writing, sharing time together. So many of us seek reunion with our birth parents when we're adults. What if we had been able to know our birth parents our whole lives? Would that have been better? Worse? Given the choice, would we choose openness, or would we just rather not know?

Coming from a closed-adoption experience, I am fascinated by open adoption. While it seems like it is intended as a step toward making the adoption experience better—after all, it takes away the secrecy and shame—I wonder if it is better, or if it's the same issues just packaged in a new way. And have we created a whole new set of issues that we didn't have in the closed adoption system?

I feel like I've experienced open adoption in a small way. I've been in reunion with my birth mother, Kate, for 23 years, since I was 18. So while I've had her in my life for longer than I've not had her in my life, it still has only been as an adult. I didn't know her when I was growing up. And that's the part that pulls at me about open adoption. You see and get to know your parents, but you don't have them as your parents.

It took a long time and a lot of work for Kate and me to get to the point where we have a good, solid relationship. We got here after a long haul of going through the reunion process. I was able to explain my hurt, my abandonment, my anger with her—all the issues I have that are a result of her choice. But I had those discussions with her as an adult. What would it have been like if I was a child? Would I have been able to talk to her about those feelings as I experienced them? Can you go through something traumatic and process it at the same time?

A short time ago, I had the opportunity to interview a birth mother who had just recently relinquished her child for adoption and will know him through open adoption. She was very frank in talking about her experience. It gave me the opportunity to wonder what it would be like to be an adoptee in an open adoption vs. being an adoptee in reunion. How is it the same and how is it different?

However, when I wrote a post about the interview for Lost Daughters, it spurred a lot of debate. I was shocked by how passionately people reacted. I imagine that hearing about a birth mother who is satisfied relinquishing her child for adoption can be disturbing and that Lost Daughters would seem like a strange place to post such a thing. Why would an adoptee want to discuss adoption with a birth mother who had just voluntarily relinquished her child?

For me, it was an opportunity to get the point of view of my birth mother 41 years ago when she relinquished me. Talking to my birth mom now, I know she wishes she'd kept me, wishes she'd found a way. I also know, though, that at the time she gave me up, she felt very satisfied with her choice. So, for me this interview was a way to go back in time to talk to the birth mom looking ahead vs. being in reunion, looking back and knowing what it has been like after the fact.

Adoption exists. Not all parents want to raise their children. The more we can question, explore and understand the experience, the more opportunity we will have to shape the future of adoption into a way that's better.

Finding My Family

By Nikki Mairs-Cayer Pike

Like most adoptees, I thought about my mother while growing up. I wondered what she looked like, speculated about her interests and personality, and hoped that she thought about me as well. During my college years, I fantasized about her finding me. My version went something like this: knowing that I had reached adulthood, she would eagerly call the adoption agency to let them know she was ready to make contact with me. The agency would locate my adoptive parents, who in turn would let me know that my mother wanted to meet me. That was the perfect scenario in my young adult mind because it removed responsibility from me as the finder, making me nothing more than the innocent one being found. My imaginary scenario, however, never played out. I briefly considered searching for her in my mid-20s when I was pregnant with my first child, and then again a few years later as I approached age 30. But each time those thoughts pushed their way into the forefront of my mind, I pushed them back down to the guarded place in my wounded adoptee psyche—the place that kept me relatively safe from my paralyzing fear of rejection, disruption, and disloyalty.

In September 2009, at the age of 39, I stumbled upon an article highlighting a handful of states allowing adult adoptees access to their original birth certificates (OBC). I was surprised to see my birth state listed. In fact, I'm not entirely sure I even knew that such a document existed. I only knew for sure that I had an amended birth certificate that listed my adoptive parents as my "mother" and "father." I proceeded to the website listed in the article, followed a series of links, and before I knew it, I was holding the short application for my OBC in my hands. And then I tucked it away for three months, before finding the courage to move forward.

My original birth certificate arrived on December 24, but being busy with out-of-town guests visiting for the holiday, we neglected to bring in the mail. Seriously, of all days to forget the mail! The following afternoon, Christmas Day, my husband came inside from checking the mailbox, and handed me an envelope from the State of Maine. I knew immediately what it was, so in a quest for privacy, I ran upstairs to my bathroom. I secured a spot on the edge of the bathtub, where I quickly but carefully opened the envelope and removed its precious contents. I can still remember my trembling fingers and racing heart as I unfolded that piece of paper. My eyes fell immediately on her name. My. Mother's. Name. Not only was her name typed, but I could see her signature. Other pieces of information were listed, like her age, hometown, and city of birth. But it was finally knowing her name, after 39 years of not knowing, that literally took my breath away. What an amazing gift to receive on Christmas Day!

Thanks to the wonders of the Internet, it only took me about 24 hours to find my mother, or the woman I was 99% sure was her. It was almost too easy the way the pieces were falling right into place. I was simultaneously excited and terrified, among a million other emotions that I couldn't quite articulate. After five days of Facebook stalking, advice seeking, and soul searching, I sent a very carefully composed message to the woman I'd been wondering about all those years. Immediately after sending the message, I ran to the kitchen where my legs practically collapsed from under me. I sat on the floor for several minutes and let the realization of what I had just done fully sink in.

The hours that followed were excruciating. I continually checked to see if I had received a response, but nothing. I tried to rationalize why I hadn't heard back yet. It was New Year's Eve, after all, and she was probably out for dinner or maybe at a party. My husband gently reminded me that it had taken me almost a week to prepare myself to send that message, and it would likely take her some time to process this information as well. After 39 years, she probably never expected to hear from me. I needed to be patient. Yeah, right.

Twenty hours later, at 11:30 a.m. on New Year's morning, the message I had been waiting for appeared in my inbox. Again with a racing heart and shaking hands, I read the first line of her response, "Hi Nikki—yes, I am her." I read and re-read her entire message. It was warm and friendly, and delivered perfectly. She agreed to answer any questions I had for her, and she wanted to know everything about me that I was willing to share. She said that giving me up was "heartbreaking and life changing," which I found both sad and comforting.

We wrote back and forth for the next several days, answering each other's questions and sharing various details about ourselves. I would wait with giddy anticipation each day, knowing that with every email I received, something new would be revealed. With each new piece of information, I was becoming more real, more whole. I discovered that she is left-handed like me, something I always wondered. We are the same height and have the same blood type. We share an affinity for list making, and we both separate our M&M's by color before eating. We enjoy the same music, prefer our apples sliced, and both have a crazy-good memory for dates.

I got my blue eyes from my father, who passed away unexpectedly in March 2005 at the age of 53. I missed knowing him by 4 years and 9 months. My mother and father were high school sweethearts, but eventually broke up after I was born, and both went on to marry other people. My mother and her husband had two daughters together, 7 ½ and 10 years younger than me. My father and his ex-wife had two children together, a son and a daughter, only 3 and 4 years younger than me.

The most shocking piece of information came a few days after our first contact. My mother told me that she and my father had another child together 20 months after I was born. I have a full sister! She was also placed for adoption, and our adoptive parents unknowingly gave us the same first name. My sister found our parents in the fall of 1991 when she was just 19, back when I was merely fantasizing about being found. That news made my head spin and filled me with regret. Why hadn't I searched sooner? The fog of denial that had served to protect me for 39 years was starting to lift. The severity of my loss was becoming more and more apparent. My grief was beginning to surface.

My mother and I continued to grow closer during the months that followed. We talked on the phone, and spent hours chatting on Facebook, really getting to know each other. We discovered some amazing coincidences, like the fact that she and my adoptive brother lived in the same small town, though didn't know each other. My husband and I had spent time at my brother's place every summer since we married in 1993, just minutes from her home. It was possible that we had passed each other on the street or sat close by in a restaurant.

The most devastating information that she shared with me was the truth about my birth and surrender. It was not her decision to give me up. She loved me, and she wanted to keep me. She held and took care of me for the 4 days we were together in the hospital. The decision to place me for adoption was made by her mother, and by society. In 1970, pregnant teens were often sent away to live out the last few months of their pregnancy in hiding. They were told that their baby would be better off being raised by a married couple who could provide the stability of a two-parent home. Young mothers were promised that they would forget the baby they gave away, and assured that they would one day marry and have more children. My mother did get married years later and she did have two more daughters, but she never forgot the two she lost.

After communicating with my mother and siblings for four months through email, online chats, phone calls, and texts, I flew to Maine to meet them in person. To say that I was excited and anxious as I boarded the plane on that April day doesn't even begin to capture the enormity of what I was feeling. Upon landing, I got situated in my rental car and made the 45 minute drive from the airport to my mother's house. The experience was surreal. I couldn't quite believe I was about to meet her face to face. In less than an hour, I would be looking into the eyes of the woman I had been separated from for almost 40 years. I pulled into her driveway at 2:30 p.m. and she immediately walked outside to greet me. It's kind of a blur to me now because I was so nervous, but I think we said hello to each other. We were both smiling, and we embraced immediately. After that long, wonderful hug, we went inside and talked for hours.

The next day, I met three of my sisters, along with my mother's older brother and younger sister. I found myself staring at each of them, searching their faces for resemblances and familiarity. My face is shaped like my mother's, but my coloring is more like that of my uncle's. When I looked at my sister, I saw my oldest son's eyes looking back at me. It's difficult to explain the mixture of emotions I felt that beautiful spring day as I sat on the deck with my newly found family. I was happy— enjoying their stories and soaking up their laughter. But I was also sad. This was my family, yet they were virtually strangers to me.

Well, it's been a few years since that first meeting, and I've since met the rest of my siblings, aunts, uncles, nieces, nephews, and many of my cousins. In fact, I have spent a lot of time with and become very close to several members of my first family. Everyone has been incredibly welcoming and accepting. I am lucky for that—not all adoptees are met with that kind of warm embrace. I'm genuinely happier than I've ever been in my life, and I feel a completeness that I never expected. It's also been hard, though. Very Hard. For me, reunion unlocked the door to a whole lot of repressed and deeply buried grief, and opened my eyes to the enormous loss that surrounds adoption. There are days when I feel completely swallowed up by the sadness of what I lost. Nevertheless, there are also days when I am able to revel in the pure joy of what I've found.

The Dream

By Samantha Franklin

"But there's a story behind everything... behind all your stories is always your mother's story, because hers is where yours begins."

—Mitch Albom, *For One More Day*

In her book, The Sound of Hope, Anne Bauer writes, "The day I realized I had two mothers, I was cut in half . . . One half of myself resided here with my family, and the other half was lost, lost to a shadowy woman floating somewhere out there in the world. You see, I'm adopted."

Growing up, I never let myself even think about my natural mother, so when I began dreaming about her as an adult, it began a whole new journey. With the blessing of my family, I searched and found her when I was in my early 20s. It was her mother, my grandmother Carolyn, who shared the devastating news that my mother had passed away while also searching for me. Her name was Norma Carol.

I was born Baby Girl Lowe during the '60s, when young, unwed mothers endured great shame—the Baby Scoop Era. They were told that giving up their babies for adoption would somehow redeem them, and us as well. They were supposed to "forget" and "move on," but most never could, including my mother.

On her deathbed, she made her family promise to never forget her only child, whom she knew would someday return. She wasn't allowed to see or hold me after giving birth and was led to believe she had given birth to a boy. But it was a daughter, me, who came back, 10 years too late.

I spent most of my 20s numb, stuffing down disenfranchised grief, especially after my mom who raised me was diagnosed with the same type of cancer that took Norma's life. Suddenly, I was terrified of losing both my mothers to this horrid disease. Mom not only endured months of chemo and radiation, but also a bone marrow transplant, never losing faith and teaching me important lessons in perseverance and trust. We just celebrated her 82nd birthday and 15 years as a survivor.

In my 30s, I could breathe again, and as I connected with other adoptees and first mothers who were sharing their experiences, I began dreaming of my mother.

One of those dreams is so special: I found myself in Norma's living room, looking out her window, and there, to my surprise, was the familiar site of my childhood neighborhood. Overcome, I turned and realized she had been with me all along. As she reached out, took me in her arms, and held me, she whispered words in my ears, words that empowered me, preparing me for life. Never before had I felt such a nurturing embrace. I never wanted to let go.

Then she said, "You know, Samantha, I can't complete you . . . " and at this, her voice trailed off. My heart sank as she pulled away, picked up her things, and walked out the door. The little girl in me stood there sobbing, helpless, trying so hard to wish her back.

Somehow, her embrace remained a part of me. I felt stronger and bigger, through even the unbearable sadness of watching her go. Then, looking down, I noticed she had left her keys there on the table. For me. They immediately brought comfort to my heart, as I knew I would someday see her again, even if in eternity. She had left me my name and a confidence that filled my grieving heart with strength.

As it was for a fellow adoptee named Moses who hid in the desert, this dream was truly a "burning bush" experience. Moses asked God, "Who am I?" and God said, "I am the God of your fathers, Abraham, Isaac and Jacob." God restored his identity and his lineage. Then God said, "Take off your shoes, for the ground you stand on is Holy." (My shoes even had names: Fear and Shame.) Moses found his destiny wrapped up in both his families and a purpose only fulfilled as he journeyed back to the place of his birth.

My uncle Ronnie says that my son reminds him a lot of Norma Carol. Life somehow has a way of coming full circle. I am whole, no longer cut in half. I am so thankful for motherhood and very blessed to be on this journey called Life with all of my fellow adoptees.

In Search Of

By Karen Pickell

—Lines in italics are thread titles found on the
"Search for Birthparent or Adoptee" forum
at www.adoption.com.

The infant internet revealed a brood of lost babies,
now grown, still wanting their mommies.

*BABY GIRL SEARCHING FOR MOM, SYRACUSE NY
JULY 30th 1974*

Did I look because I wanted mine?

*baby boy, born in Buffalo on 11/6/70, blue eyes,
blond hair, could I be yours?*

I'd thought of her.

*Looking for birthmom. 5/16/58 Hope Cottage
Dallas. You were 16.*

She shadowed me, whispering what might have
been.

*Born 12/03/69 12:06pm, Brooklyn Jewish Hosp Med
Cntr...Who am I?*

But Dad carried a photo of toddler me in his wallet
until the day he died.

Am I part of your family?

Did I seek an alternate family, in case the current one failed me?

Looking for Anyone, I was born 2-22-81 Bell Co, KY

Wouldn't we all like to have that option?

virginia born girl, 01-19-52 yearning to locate birthmom

If you mourned the mother you never remembered, it might make sense.

Need to know the missing piece

The endless list of messages from other babies was a gruesome crash from which I couldn't avert my eyes.

baby girl born 4-20-77 looking for birth mother please help

Twelve hundred pages of messages from my people.

1938 female born md looking for her birth mother or father

I was one of the lost.

Adult adoptee searching for her bio-parents, 5/14/64 Pontiac MI

My children were descendants of the lost.

Child of adoptee looking for birth grandparents, twins born 9/11/1949 Denver Colorado

Mom always figured I would be the one to search, with my questions about things no one else questioned.

looking for bmom, my DOB 5/11/85 born in NC help!

She knew she couldn't give me everything I needed. I knew I was not the daughter of her dreams.

5/24/77 Ohio looking for family please HELP!!!!

Not her fault, nor mine.

Help me find my Mom please

Mother Nature cannot be denied.

ISO birthmom URGENT. My DOB 8/19/81

I don't blame Mom for fearing I would leave her behind.

Female adoptee DOB 8-19-1950 searching for Bparents/Bsiblings

And it's not Dad's fault I waited so long.

w/f/1967/NJ still in search for birth family

Is there a right time to hurt the ones you love? Is there a wrong time to love yourself?

93

i am lost what do i do

The need to know was primal. It didn't matter what I would find.

Desperately Searching For Birth Parents Before Deployment To Iraq

I did not seek to replace.

Is There Any Way To Find My Birth Father--please All Ideas Send My Way!!!!

I wanted to find what was already mine.

adoptee born 10/1/74 in PA wants to find family

And to erase my children's questions before they needed to be asked.

Mom was born March 1, 1918 looking for info in her adoption

I didn't realize the company I kept.

Are you looking for me? 06/27/1979

So many lost.

Adoptee 12/21/1976 St Louis, MO searching...

So many questions.

Why is no one searching for me??

Trials & Triumph

Accepting My Adoptee Fate, and How That Differs From "Moving On"

By Rebecca Hawkes

Lately, I've noticed a shift in how I perceive my adoptee experience. It's possible that I have moved into the acceptance phase of grieving my adoption-related losses. I am feeling lighter, more balanced, and holding a greater appreciation for all that my experiences have brought me. As an adoptee who has struggled to make sense of what it means to be a member of two families, I am perhaps more comfortable with duality, complexity, and ambiguity than I might otherwise have been. I tend to see things through the lens of "both/and" rather than "either/or." I've come to appreciate this about myself, to view it as part of what I have to offer the world.

The following words, written by my fellow Lost Daughter contributor Julie Stromberg, resonate strongly with me:

"Adoptees will never not be adopted. But we can live our lives. We can take our unique life experience and allow it to make us compassionate beings. We are worthy of both giving and receiving love."

As do these words from Journey of the Adopted Self by well-known adoptee and author Betty Jean Lifton:

"One cannot annul the fact that one was given up by one clan and taken in by another; one can only see the consequences of that fact in a new light that illuminates what happened in a healing way."

Part of the healing process takes place when adoptees are able to accept that what happened, happened: it was their existential fate to be surrendered by one mother at birth and raised by another. To accept that, with all the relief of finding out who they are, there will always be the pain of that special history.

I like these words for the most part, but I've also noticed that I cringe a little at the line about accepting my existential fate. Let me unpack that.

I have known situations in which adoptee or first-parent expressions of pain were countered with platitudes, such as "everything happens for a reason" or "it's all part of God's plan." But these platitudes are rarely a comfort to the person in pain.

I have also met with the attitude that adult adoptees should "move on" or "get over it" or "stop dwelling in the past." This is not easy for us to do, though. Our "past" is our history, our identity, our connection to family. What's more, for those of us adopted in infancy, our trauma happened at such an early age that we have no pre-traumatized self to return to as a norm. Another complicating factor is that adoption-related pain is not commonly acknowledged as valid as a result of the mostly positive view of adoption that is held by the general public. Pain that is regularly invalidated is harder to release.

However, as I sit with Lifton's words, I realize that she isn't asking me to "move on" or to accept that my life has worked out for the best. Her words are not about "better" or "worse," but rather are a simple acknowledgment that what happened, happened and cannot be undone. This works for me. Something bad occurred; I was separated from my original family at a tender age. I have struggled because of this separation, and I will struggle likely still. In the words of my sister blogger, I will "never not be adopted."

And yet I am also OK. I am a survivor, with a survivor's strengths and gifts. Accepting my existential fate doesn't mean viewing adoption through rose-colored glasses. It doesn't mean that I won't speak my mind, tell my story, or work for change in a system that I view as deeply flawed. It doesn't imply turning a blind eye to the pain that I, and others, have endured. To the contrary, advocating for change is a big part of the fate I am embracing!

You might ask what has taken me so long to reach this understanding. The answer is that there simply was no short cut. There never is. The only way to reach dry land, in my experience, is to slog through the muck.

The Papers

By Mila C. Konomos

Excerpt from my adoption records:

List locations of child as far back as known, beginning with most recent:

4/3/1975: The baby was deserted by her mother after she was born at Shin, Young Soon Clinic and later Dr. Shin, Young Soon found her.

4/8/1975: Was referred by Dr. Shin, Young Soon to David Livingstone Adoption Programme. ...

... Why was the child placed in the original orphanage?

Found abandoned.

Child's response at time of placement.

None. ...

... Recommendation: Adoptable.

* * *

I was 15-years-old. My mom was driving us to the grocery store.

"Hey, Mom, do you know anything else about my adoption?"

She was quiet for a moment. "Like what, Sweetie?"

"I don't know, like what happened and everything."

"Well, let's see. We think perhaps your biological mother may have come from a middle class family."

"Why?"

"Well, at the time lots of babies were abandoned on the street or at police stations, but you were actually born in a clinic."

"Did my biological mother abandon me at the clinic?"

"You know she gave you up so that we could have you. You know your father and I chose you. You were the exact little girl we wanted. You're so special. You know that, don't you?"

* * *

Once we got back to the house, as we were unloading groceries, I asked my mom if I could see my adoption papers. She looked at me somewhat puzzled. "Sure, sure, when your dad gets home, we'll sit down together and take a look."

* * *

That evening, once Dad got home from work and after dinner, the three of us sat down at the table. An old, heavy-looking folder the color of baby excrement lay on the dark wooden table. It lingered between us like a giant rectangular stone separating my parents and me, as though the table was going to cave in beneath its weight. The emotion among us made me think of crusty red meat buried in the back of the freezer.

My dad pulled the folder toward him and started flipping through sheets of paper. My mom glanced at me sideways as both she and my father scanned the papers in the folder. They whispered to one another. I strained to hear their words: "...that one should be okay... I don't know, that might upset her...that might be helpful..."

I imagined myself snatching the folder and all of its contents from their hands:

I run up the stairs to my bedroom. I slam the door. Lock it. I fall to the floor with the folder in my arms. I'm shaking.

I set the folder down on the carpet. Slowly, I lift each sheet of paper, one by one. They sound delicate and soft, like leaves caught up in a breeze. I set them all down side by side, until my entire bedroom floor is covered in a quilt of documents.

Suddenly, a gale of wind twirls through my room and picks up all the sheets of paper like a dress. The dress floats through the room up to the ceiling and back down. Then it circles me, and suddenly I hear a voice. I look up, and there is a woman in the dress. I cannot see her exactly, but she is there. Her form is there, and her hair shimmers in and out as the light dances toward her and away from her.

Just as she is about to speak, all of the papers fall to the floor in a disheveled pile.

And I notice that I am crying.

* * *

Later that night, I lay tucked away in my bed. I squeezed my eyelids shut and tried to concentrate.

101

A few words flashed in and out of my mind like blinking lights: *Found abandoned. Clinic. Deserted. Her mother.* I pressed my fingertips to my temples and shook my head. As much as I tried to remember, just as much did I want to forget.

Why my Opinions About Adoption Changed

By Deanna Doss Shrodes

My opinion of adoption has changed over time. What caused me to re-think my former opinion was ... wait for it ... thinking.

Yes. That's really what it was.

I had a few decades to think. Particularly during the ones when I was having children.

I allowed my mind to go there.

THERE.

Most adoptees know where THERE is.

Once you have your own kids it's almost impossible to not go THERE.

It's the place you tried to block out in your mind so many times over your lifetime because you're not ready to go there emotionally. It's a horrible, scary place where you contemplate how a woman, who you've been told all your life "loved you so much and wanted you to have a better life," placed you with strangers.

Letting your mind go fully THERE to the reality that you were taken from your mother's arms and placed with strangers will knock you out on the couch for the weekend—with a few boxes of Kleenex, a carton of Ben &Jerry's, and a bottle or two of wine if you're a drinker. I'm not a drinker, so I had a few cartons of Ben &Jerry's and a few bags of potato chips.

When I was expecting my own children, thoughts of adoption defied what I felt and experienced. Each time I birthed another child, gently cradled them in my arms in the hospital and nursed them at my breast for the first time while watching them contentedly drift off to sleep, I experienced a jolt. Breaking through each of these extraordinary experiences with my three children was the unyielding thought, "Dear God, how in the heck did adoption ever happen to me?"

Having my own children forced me to go THERE. I tried to block it out. But it always ascended again in my soul, relentlessly screaming, "How? HOW?"

I went THERE little by little, never gaining an understanding of how a mother comes to that point.

As a Christian, I looked to the Bible. It seemed to agree with me when it came to my confusion over my birth mother's decision.

"Can a mother forget the baby at her breast and have no compassion on the child she has borne? Though she may forget, I will not forget you!"-- Isaiah 49:15

There was a reminder that God wouldn't forget me. But I wanted so bad to believe that my birth mother wouldn't either. And until 1993, I didn't know whether she did or not. The years of waiting before reunion to find out threatened to emotionally kill me.

I thought, "There has to be something more to this. Women just don't 'forget' even if the Bible says they may forget. May is not do; may is not shall; may is not will; may is not absolute; may is not definite."

May is may.

Definition of may: Used to express possibility or opportunity.

May is a possibility, not a probability.

I wasn't ever in the situation my birth mother was in—the one which caused me to have to go THERE in small steps over years time to try to wrap my brain around why she relinquished me. It took time to come out of the fog. I started studying, researching and trying to get a feel for what life was like for unmarried, pregnant girls in America in the 1960s.

I found out about something called the Baby Scoop Era. I learned that I was a Baby Scoop baby. Researching what happened to these women was so disturbing to me I could only read a few sentences at a time before I'd step away from my computer and think, "Oh my God... that's MY birth mother. That's ME. That's us. Okay... okay... okay... back away from the computer Deanna... get your gym shoes on... go for a walk or ride your bike..."

I chose this option of exercise in my more sane moments, instead of gorging on Chunky Monkey and barbeque ridges.

I could only take going THERE by allowing my mind to actually digest the evils of the Baby Scoop Era in very small doses.

Many people believe we need to be mindful of, and apologize for, past injustices in the world, suchas slavery and the Holocaust. I agree. And so I'm thinking, when are we as a nation going to rise up and ask forgiveness of the millions of women who suffered in the Baby Scoop Era? Because I'm waiting. I'm waiting for a Presidential proclamation or a day reserved to honor the women who endured this abomination. And not only does an apology not appear to be on the horizon, but in my experience, people look at you like you've just stated a belief in extraterrestrial beings or Area 51 when you say the words Baby Scoop Era.

I mentioned the existence of the Baby Scoop Era to someone recently, and they told me to my face that I was crazy. That this Baby Scoop thing is some fictitious happening trumped up by angry adoptees. Well, you know, there are idiots out there that think the Holocaust didn't exist either!

Some people that I have discussed this with don't view the Baby Scoop Era as an atrocity because no Baby Scoop babies were aborted. They ask, "What's the problem?Was it really that big of a deal to give the kid to someone else or even coerce them to relinquish? Especially when it's determined that a married couple can give them so much more than this single girl who doesn't know her head from a hole in the ground?

It should be noted simply for clarification that in addition to having a huge issue with the Baby Scoop Era, I'm also pro-life. If I ran the world, a lot of changes would take place. However,I decided to resign as General Manager of the Universe. I'll leave it to Roseanne Barr to try to run the world, or at least the USA.

So, I went THERE for such short spurts of time because it's so disturbing to me. There's much work to do for adoption to reform and center around the child instead of the agency. Not the adoptive parents. It grieves me to think about how slow reform comes, and how many children are affected in the meantime while we wait for wrongs to be righted.

106

My opinions changed about adoption because I got brave for a moment. And then I got brave for a little bit longer. Before long, I was opening my mind for a stretch of time long enough to examine the issues in a totally honest light, away from all the propaganda I had ingested over decades of time. When I dared to seek truth, I discovered that everything that had always been banged into my head and shoved down my throat just didn't add up.

I was told for so many years by well-meaning people that my mother loved me enough to "let me live." I accepted that without thinking things through, and was always so grateful I wasn't an abortion. As a young adult, I traveled ministering in churches and would even get up in front of audiences and testify, thanking God that I wasn't aborted. I even thanked my birth mother for "letting me live" on the first day of our reunion. Then I felt so silly when she responded that she never considered anything else, and furthermore abortion was not even legal until 1973.The script I'd been so dutifully performing my whole life didn't work anymore. I've since come to realize that adoption and abortion are two separate issues entirely.

I also went THERE to realize that all this "be-grateful-she-let-you-live" crap was meant to make me feel better, but it simply wasn't true. At some point, I had to grow up. That was hard in itself because adoptees aren't encouraged as a group to grow up. We're forever treated as children as society currently withholds our personal information that is rightfully ours, starting with the first legal document assigned to us as human beings. Our birth certificates are supposed to be a 100% factual piece of paper declaring who birthed us and all other details of the first day of our existence. This is information they think we're better off not knowing, even though the rest of the entire world knows this information about themselves and smugly thinks it's fine we don't. Some believe it's for everyone's own good that we are in the dark, even if we might be predisposed to breast cancer, heart disease, or diabetes. Even though we have to explain this every time we go to the doctor. No biggie, right?

Maturing means being confident enough to identify real issues and deal with them. For me, this involved discovering my identity and first family whether those in authority wanted me to or not. And going after my truth. And refusing to be denied.

It was time to allow my mind to accept that it was never about her "letting me live." God, that hurt. I wanted it to be some amazingly noble story that the powers-that-be wanted me dead, but she saved me from destruction because she loved me so much. Why couldn't she be the Wonder Woman I had envisioned from childhood, saving me from the jaws of death?

The reality of the story is she was in a hot mess because I existed.

The reality is that she was afraid of her father and other authority figures who "knew better."

The reality is that she was frightened out of her mind.

The reality is that she had no idea where to turn or what to do.

The reality is that she had to figure out what to do about me.

The reality is that I was a problem to solve.

And in the end, she followed the path that millions of other girls in that era who were pregnant and not married were coerced to do.

Warning: Going THERE and accepting all this truth may send you to lay in what appears to be a melancholy coma in your bed and watch Lifetime movies for three days at a time—while ordering takeout, not showering, and staying in the same striped Victoria's Secret PINK pajamas. Not that I've done it or anything.

So, my experience was the classic Baby Scoop Era, domestic, closed adoption. My view has changed over time, through a combination of many factors. Learning more truth about the circumstances of my birth, researching adoption practices then and now and hearing other adoptees' experiences have contributed to my change of mind.

My views on adoption reform are many, but to close these thoughts, I'll put my wish list as concisely as I can in "Deanna's 10 Not-So-Quick-And-Easy-Steps to Adoption Reform":

1) No secrets. Period. Adoptees should grow up with absolutely no secrets.

2) Original birth certificate. No exceptions.

3) For those who have an overwhelming itch to adopt, they can scratch it by considering adoption through the foster care system where there are

currently half a million children in America alone in need.

4) Adoption of an infant should be a last resort, not a first response. The first goal should be family preservation. Every attempt possible should be made to keep mother and baby together. When a girl or woman says, "I'm pregnant," our first words in response should be: "How can I help you?" not "Have you considered adoption?"

5) When an adoption must take place, it should center around the child. Too many people adopt to fill their needs, not a child's. When a parent—birth or adopted--parents to fill their own needs, they place unrealistic expectations on a child to fulfill their needs. This is very unhealthy and places an enormous, unfair burden on the child.

6) For an adoption agency to remain licensed, the provision of lifetime counseling for adoptees should be a requirement. There are billions of dollars a year flowing through the adoption industry. With all the money flowing through the system, this is a legitimate request. Many agencies offer ongoing counseling to birth mothers, even after the adoption is finalized. They don't typically provide this for adoptees. Perhaps one reason is that with the provision of lifetime counseling, they would have to admit to prospective adoptive parents that post-adoption issues are real and prevalent. It would undoubtedly shatter the false perception for adoptive parents that children are so resilient and adoption won't affect their child as

long as they shower them with plenty of unconditional love.

7) Post-adoption issues are real. Adoptive parents, yes, I know you think things are fine. Yes, I know they never say anything. Yes, I know they never bring anything up. Make the counseling available, please. They probably won't say anything to you. Because they don't want to go THERE.

8) Intermediaries shouldn't exist. Let flesh and blood talk to one another unhindered, please. They've been apart long enough. Let them talk. Let them connect. Give them their rightful information and let them be. You just mess things up. You don't improve anything. Really. They can manage this just fine without you. Even as educated as you are. Please give these relatives (yes, that's what they are) space to decide whatever they're going to do with you out of the way.

9) Non-identifying information shouldn't even exist. Adoptees have a right to know the specific details about where they came from, who they came from, their medical history, and anything else that pertains to them personally.

10) No secrets. Did I mention there should be absolutely NO secrets?

How Do We Mend the Hoop

By Trace A. DeMeyer

Years ago I was embarrassed to say I was adopted. I did not feel lucky. I did not have a clue that my adoption hurt me so badly its tentacles reached into every aspect of my life, even as an adult. My hoop, my connection to my ancestors, was broken by my adoption.

The hoop symbolizes the never-ending circle of life, which starts with birth, then goes to maturity, then to old age and death, with the completion of the hoop in rebirth here or in the spiritual world. The individual who has his life in order stands in the center of the hoop to see, to understand, and to be guided by the various paths of life around him. The best compliment one can pay an individual is to say that he stands in the center of the hoop of life or that he lives on the correct path of life. *

I ached to know my own mother, the woman who created me.

One expert wrote, "Loss of the most sacred bond in life, that of a mother and child, is one of the most severe traumas and this loss will require long-term, if not lifelong, therapy."

Really? No one helped me with this. I had therapy twice. The counseling I received in my 20s or 30s concerned my dysfunctional childhood, yet all my issues stemmed from my adoption wound and loss. The therapists missed it or didn't inquire or connect the dots. Why is that?

For close to 20 years, on my own I searched and simply wanted to find answers and the truth. I made calls before I showed up anywhere; I did not disrupt anyone's life. If I was invited to meet relatives, I went. This year alone two cousins have filled giant gaps in my ancestry. Prayers are answered, even the unspoken ones.

I can see how adoption loss can last a lifetime. Some of my friends are stalled with sealed adoption records, not knowing which tribe is theirs, and suffer greatly with grief and depression. For them, I wrote my memoir One Small Sacrifice as a journalist and adoptee, and now I maintain a blog for other American Indian adoptees raised by non-Indians. For those who attempt to open their own adoption or simply want to understand, I explain many stages, steps I had taken: some good, some hard.

Sharing stories is how we heal, how we mend the hoop.

Even now there is persistent rampant poverty in Indian Country. Even now it isnot easy being Indian, on and off the reserves. However,it is definitely better to know who you are, which tribe, and not live in a mystery. Someone needs to build a bridge for these adoptees. Open records will accomplish this.

It is hard to admit, but adoptees with Indian blood find out soon enough their reservations are closed to strangers. Without proof, without documents, you are suspect. We don't always get our proof since state laws prevent it. Just one Minnesota tribe, White Earth, decided to call out to its lost children/adoptees; this made news in 2007. Just a few adoptees showed up. Why? Adoption records are still sealed in Minnesota.

America's Indian Adoption Project was not publicized or well known, just like a few more secrets I found out. Congress heard Indian leaders complain in 1974: "In Minnesota, 90 percent of the adopted Indian children are placed in non-Indian homes."

I was born in Minnesota.

For any adoptee going back to her tribe requires a special kind of courage. Adoptees know this. Rhonda, a Bay Mills tribal member and adoptee friend of mine, was told early on to be happy, be white. Ask yourself, how would you react? When did Indian Country become such a bad place to be from? How did this happen?

My mission is to find these answers and build new bridges. It is time to mend the hoop for all adoptees.

*grandfathersspirit.com

Legitimacy

By Joy Lieberthal Rho

I love blue eyes. I love hazel eyes. I even love brown eyes. Mine, though, are so dark, you can't even see the pupil. I became aware of this during eighth-grade science class when we had to watch how light affects our pupils—my partner couldn't see anything. No change was visible. Yet another reason I didn't love my eyes. We always want what we don't have.

If you asked me when I was a senior in high school who I wanted to marry, I described a man who was tall, blonde, and blue-eyed. I wanted that sort of American look, along with a slim percentage of a chance my future child would have light eyes and wavy hair. Never in a million years could you have convinced me that I would fall in love with, let alone marry, a Korean man. OK, his hair is uncannily curly! But alas, my boys have straight, dark hair and the darkest of eyes. I adore that about them now, but back then, children who looked like me were not even glimmers in my mind's eye.

Fast forward to my life as a post-adoption social worker organizing workshops for adoptive parents. I was growing weary of the panels of adoptees coming to share their stories. I loved the stories and so did the audience. It seems a roomful of adoptive parents are ravenous for our stories and even more ravenous for our acknowledgement afterward that they are doing just the right thing because they can check off their list all the things our parents didn't do for us way back when.

However, the panels were always unstructured and too open-ended in format, leaving me feeling that we never got to the meat of how adoption impacts a person's life choices. To try and give the workshops some focus, I thought up some themes adoptees could speak and share about. Dating and relationships was just such a topic, and I knew it was by far the most personal of personal. I wanted to do this for many reasons, such as the numerous times I have had to field ridiculous comments, such as, "We are Jewish. It's important she find a nice Jewish boy, but she keeps bringing home those other Latino boys from across the tracks." Yes, you read that correctly. Finding adoptees willing to share such personal experiences as how and with whom they found love was a huge task. But find them I did, and I think I was more changed as a result than anyone.

I know I'm showing my age with what I write here. I hope I am. I hope that situations such as these won't continue to happen: There was a panelist, an Asian adoptee, who shared her experiences of dating Asian men. She was married to a Caucasian man. I rightfully guessed that the bone of contention in those past relationships was her being adopted. It usually was, and it also typically was the demise of the relationship, as no good Asian boy would date, let alone think about marrying, an adoptee. One guy's mother accused this panelist of trying to gain legitimacy as an Asian person through her son. That statement struck me dumb for a minute.

By the time I heard this panel, I had already gone through the heartache of dating a few Korean boys whose mothers refused to let me into their homes because of my being adopted. And I was already married to that wavy-haired, dark-eyed Korean man. Our very long courtship was over, and the main sticking point of our relationship—my adoption status—was water under the bridge. After all, I was self-sufficient, had gone to a good college, had a couple of degrees after my name, and was taller than my father-in-law. I kid. I seemed to have found one of the few guys who really had no worry about his parents coming around to accept me.

It was never lost on me that my relationship was a mixed-race relationship of sorts. Everything I learned about being Korean was either from a book or from my year in Korea. Even now, I work diligently to maintain my Korean and I bring objects into my home that are Korean. The consequence of my shortsightedness about what it would mean to be a Korean daughter-in-law was a few years of tears, misunderstandings, and foreheads wrinkled in confusion. Tales of Korean mothers-in-law are infamous. Just look at the blog Kimchi Mamas, which has a whole section just on mothers-in-law! While I was frustrated that I wasn't cut a little more slack for not having been raised in a Korean home, it never dawned on me that my Korean identity was legitimized by having a Korean husband. I was not more Korean because of whom I married. If that was the case, I missed that "How To" book.

I always knew I was Korean. The whole world knew it, too. It's that very part of me that caused such derision while I was growing up. Rather than clarifying my identity, being married to a Korean man has forced me to be far more vigilant in how I identify myself so I don't lose the hyphenated aspect of who I am. The American and adopted parts of me are equally essential in determining what box to put me in.

My truth back in high school was this: As an adolescent girl wanting so desperately to fit in, I believed an all-American, blonde-haired, blue-eyed boy would legitimize me as an American. He would make my Korean face disappear. No one would look at me strangely and wonder if I spoke English, if I was American enough. He would be my proof that I belonged here. How youthfully superficial was that? I see that now. These days, I can also look at my very Korean-looking sister and her tall, fair-complexioned, light-haired husband and only see love. I enjoy hearing my nephew declare that he looks more Korean than his sister. And I can now see that I found love in the form of a person who looks just like me, legitimately.

When People Leave

By Deanna Doss Shrodes

"Do you want to go up and see Pop?"

I was just a small girl, not even in school yet, when my father held my hand and led me to Pop's casket. Pop wasn't my grandfather or even a relative, he was a man in our church who everyone called "Pop."

This was the first death I ever experienced, the first funeral visitation I ever attended in my life.

"Yes, I want to see him," I said faintly. I looked at Pop and then asked my dad why he was lying there in the box.

Why he looked like he was sleeping.

If he would ever wake up.

Where he was now.

My dad patiently answered all the questions. I was told that Pop went to heaven. He would not be coming back to earth, but we would see him one day when we went to heaven.

I never said anything, but I remember thinking it over during the next few days following the visitation. I was articulate as a child, placed in advanced reading and writing in first grade. I was good at verbally communicating, singing and reciting poems in front of others since I was four years old. Yet I stayed oddly silent about these new revelations.

I was scared out of my mind.

Scared of loss.

Terrified about people going away from the world—from my world—and never coming back.

I remember a few days after Pop's funeral, I was outside playing in our fenced-in yard. I ran to the other side of the yard, to be by myself. Holding on to the fence tightly, with my knuckles turning white, I stared out into the sky, just trying to make sense of this whole idea of people going away.

I had always been told I was adopted. I don't ever remember not knowing because I was often told the story from my very infancy of how my parents came to adopt me. I knew there was a first mother who gave me to an adoption agency and went away and then my adoptive parents came and got me.

Gripping on to the fence that day, squinting into the sun, I was consumed with thoughts of death and abandonment. I remember feeling so anxious and sad. I cried and wanted to hide it. So I made no sound.

After a while, my mother opened the door and called out to me to come inside.

I was unusually subdued and she sensed something was wrong.

"What's the matter?" she said.

"Nothing," I murmured.

I never told her that, until that week, I hadn't realized people died.

I never told her that, although I wasn't close to Pop, I felt so much overwhelming fear and loss that I couldn't explain it, even as a verbose child.

I never told her the thought came to me that day that my first mother had gone away and never came back.

I never told her I was afraid that she and my dad were also going to leave and never come back.

I never told her or my father so many of my thoughts because I didn't feel the comfort level to do so. Like so many adopted kids, I kept a lot inside, at least about my adoption or things that I connected to it emotionally.

I feared my adoptive parents would leave, and actually one of them did. My adoptive dad left and filed for divorce, and our family broke apart in dysfunction. Yes, it was one of the most painful times of my life. I took the loss of our family unit doubly hard as an adoptee. The sale of my childhood home after their divorce emotionally killed me.

I can remember sitting in the family room when my mother told me the divorce was impending and she would be selling the house. She asked what I was feeling. Although at that time I was a teenager who was, in fact, preparing for a career in communication and pretty good at it, I was at a loss to verbalize what was in my heart. It was too enormous. Too ugly. I was crushed. I could only choke out through sobs, "I always thought I'd have some place I could call home and now I don't."

Loss never got easier over the years. For me, an adoptee, it is particularly hard.

I've been adopted for 47 years now. I wish I could say loss gets easier, but it doesn't.

My husband and I are in full-time ministry and have been co-pastoring for 25 years. Over these years, I have not only attended countless funerals, as a licensed minister I have officiated them. Yes, I cry, even though I am in charge. No one seems to mind, in fact it oddly endears them to me and they thank me for caring so deeply.

Sometimes people leave our church for various reasons. I feel the pain and rejection so deeply, more than anybody could ever imagine. Prayer helps a lot, but it still hurts profusely. I'm human.

Other times, people in my life move away. A few years ago my closest friend and her family moved away because of a job transfer. She didn't want to leave, but economic and career reasons dictated the move. I held my head high in front of everybody, but the morning the moving truck actually pulled away was the start of two weeks of bawling in the shower every morning before work. In a few weeks time, I was able to get up and shower without crying. It got better each day, but I had to go through the process of grief in order to correctly heal.

The reality is that sometimes our fears of abandonment come true all over again, and it hurts. It hurts so badly.

For many years I thought this was all due to my personality profile. I thought I'm an organized and regimented person who doesn't like change or goodbyes just suck. Then I realized that it's more than that. Yes, change is a challenge for most, and goodbyes are no one's favorite. But for an adoptee, these events are often triggers for what was the first, and possibly most, traumatic event of our lives.

Though it never gets easier to deal with fresh wounds, I have learned about coping skills and the importance of connection:

Familiarize yourself with the stages of grief defined by Dr. Elisabeth Kubler Ross. Recognize them, go through them, don't rush them. To heal properly from each loss we have to process it properly.

Connect with people who understand. When it comes to adoptee fear of loss and abandonment, I've found other adoptees or a therapist understand it best. At times when I've shared with non-adoptees, the response I get is, "Well, we all face loss. I mean, how is your feeling of loss any different from anybody else's? Loss is loss." All I can say to that is, it doesn't pay to argue with fools.

Be kind to yourself. You should always be kind to yourself, but during times of loss, be especially kind.

We can navigate the waters of loss without emotionally drowning. Throwing yourself the life preserver time and time again works, but it's so much easier when someone else who understands can throw you the lifeline and help pull you in.

Lost Daughters has been that place for me. This community has validated and encouraged me and provided a safe place to land. A place where I know I am not alone.

Make it Bleed

By Mei-Ling

Adoption is like an invisible wound that keeps scarring over and over again.

Truth be told, I haven't really thought about it that much. It's not that I have forgotten about "that life," more like I don't allow myself to dwell on it. It's a coping mechanism that works nicely. I don't dwell on it so it doesn't disrupt my daily life. This allows me to function properly and spend my energy elsewhere. Most days I am perfectly fine. Most days I have so many other things to think about.

Whenever I dwell on adoption, the depth of heartbreak can seriously overwhelm me.

And then it happens. Once in a while someone will suggest that I message Gege* about Skyping, or try to call internationally just to say hi. Or they will ask if I've kept in touch.

The last time I received a call from Taipei was approximately two and a half months after returning from overseas. My previous roommate had called during her lunch break to discuss a financial matter. I knew it would be daytime; I could hear the sounds of laughter in the background. A mental picture of children playing and being part of a community half a world away filled my mind's eye. Then the call ended.

That hurt.

Give me something, only to rip it away.

People seem to think it would make me feel better if I could call. They think it would help me to feel more connected to a world I'm not a part of.

They also seem to think it would comfort me to hear my mother's voice, to be able to say hi to her. Or to say anything at all.

It just makes me bleed.

*"Gege" is Mandarin for "elder brother."

Be the Trump Card

By Laura Dennis

New Year's Eve is often a time to reflect on the previous year and make resolutions for the one ahead. I have a somewhat radical suggestion: Be the trump card.

It might sound wrong, or presumptuous, or just plain bitchy, but . . . be the trump card.

The American Heritage New Dictionary of Cultural Literacy, Third Edition , defines "trump card" this way:

In general, something capable of making a decisive difference when used at the right moment; in certain card games, trump is the suit designated as having precedence over the others.

We, dear adoptees, can make the decisive difference in how our family and friends view our own reunion. Whether considering searching or not, whether found or in long-term reunion, it's all about the adoptee. We are the children in this equation.

We were the tiny babies who didn't consciously know what was happening. We are the children who, of course, loved our adoptive parents. We are the 18-year-olds whose records were available (in some states), but who were unprepared for the opened emotional wound. We are the adults who are still figuring out all of this adoption stuff.

Now, we can be the trump cards! Granted, it's a mighty selfish statement.

Full Disclosure

I have always been a people-pleaser. I'm the eldest child. I'm a typical type-A, perfectionist, control freak. Adding insult to injury, I'm adopted.

As a child, the role of perfect daughter came easily to me. I was the adoptee who was subconsciously afraid of being given back or given away. Not that it was possible, or threatened, or something I thought of deliberately. It was simply the logical extension of the narrative my adoptive parents told me: "Your birth mother loved you enough to give you up, and now we love you."

So you could give me up, too, I thought.

I was aware of my desire to fulfill my adoptive mom's dream of being a mother. I was determined to be the good child for whom she had prayed to God.

Meeting My First Mother

Reuniting with my first mother was one of the most amazing experiences of my life. Reunion filled a hole in my heart and made me question all of the decisions I'd made so far in my life. My first mother and I connected on a deep physical and emotional level.

Not only that, but my reunion was one of the first times when I realized that it was, in fact, all about me. I surprised myself in that I felt totally fine about this. From the beginning of our reunion, my first mother let me take the lead. She shielded me from her grief and she was careful to share painful pieces of information about my relinquishment little by little.

Everyone constantly asked, "How are your parents handling this?" It's a funny question, but it's one that's normal among those who know little about how hard adoption can be on the actual adoptee. Generally, I brushed off the question, answering, "They're fine." Sometimes, when I was feeling particularly sassy, I have to admit I did add, "They're not the ones reconnecting with their family after decades of waiting, you know?"

Once reunion fever set in, I stopped worrying about what my adoptive parents were going through. I didn't try to defend my search decision to people I hardly knew. This was my reunion. Feeling guilt about reuniting or trying to manage others' reactions was simply too much for me to take on.

As I've become more involved in the world of adoption blogging, I've read over and over how worried adoptees are about how their adoptive parents will feel:

"Will they think I don't love them if I search?"

"I could search, but I couldn't tell my adoptive parents, they'd be too upset."

"My natural family could never meet my adoptive family; it would be too hard for everyone."

I've seen adoptees go to extreme psychological, physical and logistical lengths to provide for the privacy, safety and emotional security of the people who raised them and of their natural families.

I admit, especially in the honeymoon period of my reunion, I believed my first mom could do no wrong. It was maddening for those close to me (friends and fiancé, not just my adoptive parents). I get it. For a time, I became a different person who was in complete wonderment at the reunion for which I'd waited my entire life.

Be the Trump Card

Yes, it is necessary to explain our perspective on adoption to those close to us kindly, gently and with emotional intelligence. But also with boundaries. With the knowledge that whatever we feel and whatever shape we want our reunions to be, it's up to us, the adoptees.

We, dear adoptees, are the trump cards in this equation.

My Birthday

By Nikki Mairs-Cayer Pike

Tomorrow is my birthday. I never used to think that my birthday affected me much when I was growing up. I mean, I always...ALWAYS...thought about my mother on that day. I figured that if there was one day of the entire year that she wondered about me, it was my birthday. However, I never connected a conscious feeling of sadness to that particular event, until about a year ago when I happened upon my second-grade report card. I was completely shocked, almost in disbelief, when I read my teacher's comment from the last grading period: "We had the problem of extreme sadness for days over school closing and now this has switched to something akin to anger. She's a deep little girl."

The final report card was dated June 17, 1978, just 4 days after my 8th birthday. My teacher's comment stopped me in my tracks, and honestly, kind of knocked the wind out of me. Maybe there was more to my childhood end-of-school-year despair than just end-of-school-year despair. I can remember the tears, the emptiness, and even the fear that plagued me, year after year, as those final days approached. I never considered it unusual because, after all, I did love school. But extreme sadness and anger? Even for a little girl who adored spelling tests and delighted in math problems, that reaction seemed a bit over the top.

Was my sadness during that time ONLY about school ending? Or did my soul always remember that it was the middle of June when I lost my mother? We spent the first four days of my life together. Without a doubt, I felt the anguish of her bewildering absence. Her familiar sound, smell, and touch were no longer there. The person to whom I had been intimately connected for nine months had disappeared. How could that experience not affect me and leave a lasting imprint on my psyche?

I suppose I'll never really know what was going on with me in June of 1978 that caused my teacher to take notice of my behavior—behavior that was clearly uncharacteristic. Maybe most years, it really was just sadness over a wonderful school year coming to an end. I suspect, though, that at least that year my little 8-year-old soul was longing, missing, hurting over something much deeper. And without the conscious memories of my loss to guide my awareness, I had no idea what that something was.

It wasn't until I found my mother 2 ½ years ago that my birthday started bothering me in a very real and obvious way. It wasn't until then that I stopped and really thought about the day I was born. My birth day. There were no excited visitors or congratulatory phone calls. No one happily snapping sweet and silly photos. My mother's joy over seeing and holding me was heavily dampened by the knowledge of what was inevitable. Five days after my birth, with no hope left of being able to keep me, she signed the relinquishment papers. Two days later, she made the long, silent ride home with empty arms.

So, tomorrow I will celebrate my birthday. And I'm hoping that by writing this stuff down and sharing it with anyone who cares to read it, this year will be different than the last two. Maybe this year I won't replay the sad events surrounding my birth over and over in my mind. This year I will try to let go of the hurt and anger that take hold during my birth week. But if that doesn't work, I'll eat lots and lots of chocolate, and wait for next week to arrive.

Oh, the Places You'll Go!

By Samantha Franklin

My first introduction to adoption poetry was a framed version of an old classic, "Chosen Child." It hung on my mother's bedroom wall right next to an ever-growing collage of my school pictures. I never understood why I hated that wall. When I entered that room, I needed to avoid eye contact with that wall, those pictures, and that poem. I couldn't understand why. I thought I hated my pictures and myself, but now I realize it was the poem.

The poem has a lot of contradictory statements, which is confusing to an adopted child. The first stanza begins: "I had to tell you, Dearest Heart, / that you are not my own." It goes on to explain how much this mother wanted and desired a baby, and how she and her child were brought together through adoption. Then in the last stanza, the poem states the child is "my baby and mine alone." How can that be?

How can I not be hers, but also hers alone? It doesn't make sense. Yet that is just one example of many double messages adoptees grapple with in a lifetime.

In order to increase the number of available babies for adoption (the commodity), we adoptees get mixed messages galore. We are a crisis— unwanted, abandoned orphans. Yet also chosen, special, lucky gifts. Our first mothers are told they are incapable, yet also heroic. Our very identities are "amended" to fulfill a role, and we're expected to cut ourselves off completely (the message of sealed records) from the identity, heritage and family line in which we were born.

Adoption is a legal contract that tries to do the impossible. "As if born to" can never replace the reality of profound loss for an adoptee, yet we are asked to live a lifetime of splitting ourselves off from our very core. We become masters at people pleasing and compliance because we are given a message that our adoption has made us "worthy." It cleansed us of being "bastards." Our original identities are "sealed" and therefore must somehow define us in shame. So, we work extremely hard to earn our place in a world where everything about us had to be amended in order for us to be accepted. What a heavy burden for any child, any human.

As a young child, I was the master homemade-card maker. I would make elaborate cards for my Mom proclaiming she was the best mother in the world. I think it was my way of trying desperately to ease the insecurity in both of us. With the words of the "Chosen Child" poem always looming, I can now understand that insecurity.

* * *

Years after my reunion with my first family, I went to an art class, which turned out to be a life-defining experience. We were asked to read the Dr. Seuss book Oh, the Places You'll Go! and then compose a poem and create a companion pastel drawing. I had never taken art before and felt that, because I had no talent, my pastel would be embarrassing at the least. But I decided to go for it.

134

After about four hours, during which it felt like time was literally standing still, I brought myself back into the real world as a different person—a person who had finally given herself permission to grieve and to shed tears over her adoption. I had always heard that art was good for the soul, that it somehow unlocked the "feeling" side of the brain, and by the time I pulled myself away from this project, I was a true believer. I vowed to take more art classes, set up a studio, and dive into this newfound, healing passion.

Five years later, here I sit without going one step further into that dream. I'm just thankful for the amazing experience of that teacher and the healing that flowed.

Oh, The Places You'll Go

You'll wake up one day and find yourself floating
on rivers of golden tears
In deep scars of black and purple, too
Streaming from your hidden view
Amidst eyes of blue.
Encircling your heart is crimson red
Blood of the fathers you never knew
Heart enshrined
Finally you'll find the real "you"
Safely hidden in this prison of blue
Your only chance now is to ride the hues
Grief unlocks the colors of life
You'll find your "purple" deep inside
after the ride
So close your eyes, and feel the depth
You'll find you're not alone

Surrounded by the throng, the unseen tears
hold on
I must visit the eyes of my forefathers
The pain of my unknown
Connect with the blood with whom I found life
love through the tears of my own.

I Am Going To Tell You a Story of What I Overcame

By Amanda H.L. Transue-Woolston

I was uncharacteristically silent on my blog when I reunited. I did not announce that I had found my original family or that I met my original mother, which is ironic because the purpose of my blog had long been to record my quest for reunion. I mused about events in popular media in blog entries during that time, staying far away from my personal narrative. I was frozen in silence from the shock of how real my story had become. I was balancing a complex spectrum of emotions that I couldn't imagine putting into words.

A year after my reunion, I wrote the stories of opening the envelope that contained my original mother's contact information, contacting her for the first time, and meeting her face to face for the first time. What I had gained throughout that first year of reunion was confidence. What I had received from both families was the reassurance that I could view, interpret and express my own story in my own voice, even when my story intersected with their stories.

At each anniversary of my reunion, I again feel the need to tell a story. It just so happened that one year, my reunion anniversary coincided with my final semester in undergrad. In a seminar class, my fellow students and I were asked to each say what we had learned throughout our academic career thus far. My academic career corresponded with the beginning of many things: my activism, my writing, my reunion, my unsealed records, and my finally embarking on the specific career path that I know without a doubt fits my passions and talents.

To express this to my fellow students, I told a short story:

In my second class here, we were given an impromptu assignment that required us to talk critically, in front of the class, about the families that raised us. I left the room in tears. I could not do the assignment. I could not talk about my family in front of the class. I have grown. The conclusions in the very papers I've written have lengthened and developed. I've come to a place where I can pull back and see a bigger picture and give meaning to tough things.

I shared how I was able to examine my experiences and myself critically and with confidence in my application to graduate school. I felt sincere gratitude for the role that my professors and peers had played in giving me support and skills to grow personally and professionally.

There is more to the story than just those few sentences I shared with my class. It is a story that exemplifies what it is like to work through a moment when being adopted is hard. It is a story that confirms that tough adoption moments can be worked through, and that it is possible and necessary to move to self-affirming conclusions.

I am going to tell you that story.

Three Years Earlier

I took a deep breath. *1, 2, 3, 4, 5.* I exhaled.
I am not going to cry.
I am not going to cry.
I looked around the classroom. No one seemed to notice me. After another deep breath, I exhaled again. The release of breath from my body sent the first few welled up tears rolling over my cheeks and onto my notebook.
Stop crying.
The professor had just asked us to do an impromptu presentation on an assignment in which we had critically evaluated the values of the family that raised us. I had interviewed my adoptive parents and grandmother and completed the written assignment. I never anticipated I would have to share about my family, especially in critique, in front of the class.
What seemed like a reasonable task for other students sent a rush of emotions to my chest and set tears burning at my eyes. Every time I attempted to lay out in my mind exactly what I was going to say, the tears threatened again. Even saying simple phrases like "my mom" and "my family taught me" to introduce the topics in my presentation felt like it would be a climb up a steep mountain.
Why?
Because *my mom* was badly hurt by me right then.
Because *my family taught me* things while my other invisible family, who was also hurting right then, never had the chance to teach me anything.

You need to understand what being publicly critical of my adoptive family represented to me in that moment. I did not want to admit that my parents are not perfect when I had already been so busy trying to prove to the world that they are perfect. Reunion, and everything that comes with it, was *my* choice and not a response to what some people might assume to be parenting failures.

The student next to me was preparing to stand up at the front of the class. It would be my turn soon.

I decided that I could not give the impromptu presentation without bawling in front of my peers. I considered telling them why sharing about my family at that time was hard. I considered attempting to do the presentation through the tears, after explaining why I was crying. I had already explained so much to those in my personal life about why I wanted to reunite. I did not want to have to keep explaining my thoughts and my heart over and over again.

I excused myself, gathered my books, quietly closed the door behind me, and walked slowly down the hallway. The tears readily flowed now. Huge, wet drops rolled down my cheeks, finding landing places on strands of my hair and on the school logo printed on my sweatshirt. I was frustrated with myself for not being able to figure out how to stop crying. I was angry for being unable to figure out how to make being adopted not be hard.

I had newly become aware of the pain and loss an entire family experienced after losing me as a member when I was surrendered to adoption. I was navigating reunion with both my maternal and paternal family members within the context of extremely sensitive conception circumstances.

I had finally learned my family medical history. At the urging of my paternal aunt and due to the significant presence of cancers in my ancestral line, I had some skin biopsies done and was awaiting the results. This was my third cancer scare in only 25 years of life.

I carried immense guilt for causing my parents to feel a wide range of positive, negative and painful emotions when I announced that I was searching for my original family.

All of these emotions were intensified by hormones. I was pregnant at the time and didn't know it. Because of infertility issues, all three of my pregnancies were a complete surprise. I miscarried a few weeks later.

These were tough circumstances present in my life at that time that adoption shot through like a cannonball, striking me right in my gut, leaving me feeling winded and sometimes defeated. It was impossible to ignore the complexity adoption brought to my life or how it intensified the process of growing as a young adult.

I was acutely aware that there were people in the world, including fellow adoptees, who had greater challenges than I did. Nevertheless, this fact did not keep the tears from falling. It is not that those who are not adopted do not have problems in life. Adoptees, like everyone else, experience tough life and family challenges. However, adoption can make these life challenges more intense and more complex, often times within an overwhelming context of loss.

I left the class and emailed an apology to the teacher. I was determined to overcome the challenges that rendered me frozen and in tears that day. There were times when I felt being adopted was easy and I didn't have to think about it. I wanted to find that person within myself and hand her these tough experiences to fix. I did not have the answers anymore.

Now

I emerge from my home on a gorgeous spring day. My screen door claps against its frame behind me as I step out into the sunlight. My children play happily in their sandbox as I clink the yard gate shut and kneel down on the fresh earth in front of me. On my knees, I wade through a mix of hostas, which have recently burst through the ground, and those stubborn wild onion weeds. Our garden soil is always rich and full of wriggling earthworms; an underground stream runs somewhere through our yard. Still, the weeds are difficult to separate from the earth. As a cold sensation soaks through my jeans, chilling my knees, I remember that it has just rained. It is always easier to pull weeds when it rains. I begin to yank the green intruders from my garden in handfuls, easily unearthing their tangled bulbs. I recall being a little girl and thinking that the rain was the earth's way of having a good cry— just as I needed to have a good cry that day in the classroom three years ago; there were some things I needed to weed out.

142

I know that sad stories can make people uncomfortable. Why bother telling one at all? Reflecting on a challenging time in life allows you to identify skills you used to survive so that you can go on to conquer other challenges. It also shows you the bigger picture of life, which is full of trials to overcome whether you are adopted or not. Can I be the hero of the story if you don't know what I conquered? Can you understand how far I have come without knowing where I have been? Can you cheer for me if you do not know what challenges me? Can you congratulate me for a job well done without knowing what I did?

Writing has helped me the most in this experience of assigning meaning to adoption in my life in early adulthood. Exploring adoption in my life helped me discover that I enjoy writing. As for the challenges that had piled up to that day, acknowledging them allowed me to tackle them. I have taken my relationships one day at a time. I followed through on the health care issues and did not test positive for skin cancer. I have learned to listen to people who identify my strengths and to those who challenge me. I began engaging in adoption discourse and reading adoption literature, both to help me understand adoption and to use that information to try to make a positive difference. It has been a process of growth and self-discovery.

The reason my personal triumphs in life are worth celebrating is that those situations were hard to begin with. Human resiliency is always worth celebrating.

I finished that class, and I went on to finish the entire program. In conjunction with graduating, I wrote a personal letter to every professor with whom I came into contact during my undergraduate social work experience. It does not matter whether I took their classes or not. If they have ever crossed paths with me and have given me feedback, I wrote to them. Every contribution, no matter how small, helped shape me into the person I have become. In each letter, I made sure to tell that professor a story. The young woman who once left class in tears has gone on an introspective and extrospective journey, and is able now to tell her story with her head held high. It is a story of a young woman who had trouble identifying her own strengths, who embarked on a seemingly endless journey of finding a place in the professional world. It is the story of a young woman who, with the guidance of her friends, educators and mentors, became empowered. It is the story of a young woman who found her original family, found even stronger bonds with her adoptive family, found her professional calling, and found herself. And she liked what she found.

When I tell you a story of what it is like to be lost, it is so you can fully understand what I mean when I tell you what it is like to be found.

I won't always tell a sad story. To be honest, it wouldn't be a reflection of my life if I always told a sad story. I do not live a sad life. I will not, however, undervalue a story just because it is sad. If I turn away from the parts of life that burn, I will never get to witness the beauty of a storyteller rising from the ashes.

About the Authors and Editors

Amanda H.L. Transue-Woolston, B.S.W., Editor

Amanda is a social worker, published author, and speaker. She has an A.A. in psychology, a B.S.W. in social work, and is currently a candidate for a master's in clinical social work. Amanda's work on adoption has appeared in multiple books, magazines, journal articles, and radio interviews, and has been presented at several conferences. She is a founding board member of the Adoption Policy and Reform Collaborative and also founded Pennsylvania Adoptee Rights and *Lost Daughters*. Amanda co-facilitates an adoption support group for anyone connected to adoption, and is a quarterly contributor to *Gazillion Voices* magazine. Amanda is best known for her internationally recognized, award-winning adoption blog, *The Declassified Adoptee*.

Julie Stromberg, Editor

Born, adopted and raised in the Northeast region of the United States, Julie reconnected with her natural parents and families in 1998. Since then, she has applied her lifelong experience as an adopted person to conducting critical analysis of global adoption practices. She holds a bachelor's degree in Journalism from Loyola University Maryland and her essays on the adoption experience and industry have been published online and in print. She writes about her personal experiences as an adoptee and adoption reform at www.lifeadopted.com.

Karen Pickell, M.A., Editor

Karen Pickell holds a Master of Arts in Professional Writing from Kennesaw State University. She has previously published poetry, nonfiction and book reviews. She serves on the board of directors of the Georgia Writers Association, as associate editor of the online literary magazine *Flycatcher*, and as an editor for the Georgia Poetry Society. Karen was born and adopted in Ohio in the late 1960s. She reunited with her birth mother in 2005 and with her birth father in 2007. She is currently working on a book about her adoption experience. In addition to being a regular contributor at *Lost Daughters*, Karen blogs about writing, editing, adoption and other topics at www.karenpickell.com.

Jennifer Anastasi, Editor

Jenn was born and domestically (United States) adopted in the late '80s as an infant in Massachusetts, a tiered access state. She searched and found her first family in 2010 with no access to her original birth certificate (she was born in a blackout year) and has been traveling the rocky road that is reunion ever since. When Jenn isn't pondering adoption and what it means to her, she can often be found curled up with a good book or dancing in her bedroom with the music blasting.

Carlynne Hershberger

Carlynne is a late discovery adoptee who was adopted by her stepfather. She is also a natural mother who lost a daughter to a coerced adoption in 1980. She found out about her own adoption six years after losing her daughter. She's been reunited with her daughter since 2002. She now blogs about adoption at *One Option Means No Choice*. She is an artist producing a series of paintings and narrative poetry about adoption called *Silent Voices* and she is currently the treasurer for Origins-USA.

Cathy Heslin

Cathy is a reunited adult adoptee living in Portland, Ore., with her husband and two children. Cathy was born in New Jersey and adopted as an infant. Cathy first reunited with her birth mother when she was only eighteen and moved across country to live with her after college. She found her birth father 10 years later. In partnership with her birth mother, she co-authored their memoir, titled *Kathleen ~ Cathleen*, which takes the reader through the parallel experience of the adoptee and birth mother over the course of two decades and the unique blended family that forms as a result. Cathy writes about adoption on her personal blog, *ReunionEyes*.

Christina Worthington

Christina is an adult adoptee in reunion with her natural mother and family since July of 2008. She was born in Massachusetts and placed for adoption six days after her birth in 1974. Christina is a full-time, corporate cubicle-dweller, mother to two children, and life partner to a very patient and understanding man. When she's not crunching numbers at work, crocheting afghans, reading a good book, or running after her kids, she's posting at her beloved blog *Out of the Fog*, and more recently, her blog *Reunited Cricket*.

Deanna Doss Shrodes

Deanna Doss Shrodes is a licensed minister with the Assemblies of God and has served as a pastor for 26 years, along with her husband, Larry, whom she met at Valley Forge Christian College where they were both students preparing for pastoral ministry. They have been married for 26 years, have three children, and live in the Tampa Bay area where they co-pastor Celebration Church of Tampa. Deanna speaks at churches and conferences internationally and is also an accomplished musician, worship leader, songwriter, and certified coach. An award-winning writer, she is a contributing author to the *Chocolate* series for women, published by Simon & Schuster, and the author of the book *Juggle: Manage Your Time, Change Your Life*. Adopted in 1966 in a closed domestic adoption, she searched and found her original mother, sister and brother and reunited with them in 1993. Deanna blogs about adoption issues at her personal blog, *Adoptee Restoration*, and also serves as the spiritual columnist at *Lost Daughters* and well as being a regular contributor at *Adoption Voices Magazine*. She is passionate about bringing hope and healing to adoptees, as well as expanding the Christian community's understanding of adoption.

Elaine Penn

Elaine is a reunited adult adoptee. Like many Americans, her adoption was a private domestic infant adoption. She was born and still resides in New Jersey with her loving husband and children. Elaine is very well known in adoption circles as an adoptee rights activist. She created and runs the popular "You Know You're an Adoptee When" page on Facebook. Elaine has also had the opportunity to tell her personal story of adoption by testifying in front of the New Jersey senate committee and was featured on the nationwide television show *Inside Edition* in 2013.

Elle

Elle is a female Korean adoptee who was relinquished for intercountry adoption two days after her birth. She was adopted to Sweden before she was three months old. She was born as the seventh and last daughter of her birth parents and has one younger birth sibling. Her brother, younger than her by five years, was also adopted from Korea. She found her birth family 10 years ago when she was 15 years old. Now in her 20s, she has visited Korea twice.

Joy Lieberthal Rho, LCSW-R

Joy holds a master's in Social Work from Columbia University. She has worked in a variety of settings, always with adoption as the focus: as a policy analyst for the Evan B. Donaldson Adoption Institute; in placement and post adoption departments for a private adoption agency; and currently, in private practice with clients touched by adoption. She co-authored the report on the The Gathering of the First Generation of Adult Korean Adoptees in Washington, D.C., and has also been published by Child Welfare League of America in their *Adoption and Ethics* series. She has created curricula for agencies and professionals on a wide variety of topics (for example, preparing for birth country visits and an overview of clinical issues in adoption) as they relate to helping families and children around adoption issues. Joy is adopted from South Korea. She came to her family just shy of her sixth birthday. She was the president of Also-Known-As, a New York based, nonprofit volunteer organization for internationally adopted people and families. She created their highly successful youth mentorship program and ran a variety of forums for adult adoptees. She was on the planning committee for The Gathering of the First Generation of Adult Korean Adoptees in 1999 as well as The Gathering in Korea in 2004. She lived in Korea for a year working in the orphanage where she once resided. During that time, she learned how to speak Korean, learned that her birth mother had been searching for her for 21 years, and learned that her identity as a Korean adopted person was a significant aspect of who she is. She has been in reunion with her birth mother since 1994. She writes a personal blog, www.adoptionechoes.com.

Karen Brown Belanger

Karen Brown Belanger is an adult adoptee activist, reformer and writer involved since 1999 in educating the world about adoption and the need for change within the system. Karen is also the author of *Assembling Self*, an adoptee's journey in self-discovery in poetry to find out who she really is, and a blog of the same name.

Laura Dennis

Laura Dennis is an adult adoptee in reunion with her maternal first family. Born in New Jersey, raised in Maryland, she considers herself a "California girl," even though she currently lives in her husband's hometown, Belgrade, Serbia, with their two small children. *Adopted Reality*, Laura's 9/11 memoir of adoption, reunion and a brief bout with insanity, is available on Amazon. She blogs about expat (adopted) mommy life.

Liberty Ferda

Liberty was born and adopted in Illinois under the closed adoption system. With an otherwise happy upbringing, she struggled with identity, due to the secrets surrounding her background and living as a mixed-race person in rural Midwest. (Her hair was a clue to her racial heritage, which her adoptive parents were not aware of.) She found her birth mother, whose background is Irish and English, through the adoption agency at age 19, and found her African-American biological father through Facebook at age 28. She received her original birth certificate from the state of Illinois in 2012, after the passage of historic legislation allowing access. She teaches English in Pittsburgh and is writing a memoir about her experiences.

Lynn Grubb

Lynn was born and adopted in Illinois in the 1960s and was raised and currently lives in Dayton, Ohio, with her husband of 22 years, Mark, and their two children (one by birth and one by adoption). Lynn holds a bachelor's degree from Wright State University and a paralegal certificate from the American Institute of Paralegal Studies. She is the policy columnist for *Lost Daughters* and is on the legislative committee of the Adoptee Rights Coalition. Lynn is a former Court Appointed Special Advocate (CASA) and is passionate about writing from a place of authenticity. She blogs at www.noapologiesforbeingme.blogspot.com.

Mei-Ling

Mei-Ling is a transracial adoptee and was adopted to a white Canadian family. She has been overseas twice and even had the chance to live with her family during her studies abroad. When she has spoken about the difficulties of a language barrier, as her family does not understand English, many people have suggested language exchanges or to continue taking classes without realizing the complexity of language beyond the classroom. She has been asked why she does not maintain much contact or use Skype to communicate. What many do not understand is that sometimes having such a fleeting connection can be far more painful knowing it will be snatched away in the end.

Michelle Lahti

Michelle is a recently reunited adult adoptee and a mother through birth and adoption. Born in the late 1960s, she was adopted as an infant in what was then a typical closed adoption. The laws of her state continue to reflect the stigma and secrecy of that time, prohibiting her from obtaining her original birth certificate without a court order. She is indebted to those who laid their souls bare as they shared their own stories and who patiently bore with her in the early years of examining her thoughts and feelings about adoption. Today she is proud to advocate for adoptee rights, family preservation, and adoption reform. You can find more of Michelle's writings at her personal adoption blog, *The Warrior Princess Diaries*.

Mila C. Konomos

Mila is a reunited Korean American transracial adult adoptee. She was born in Seoul, Korea, in 1975 and adopted six months after her birth. She is a wife and new mom. She reunited with both her Omma and her Appa in 2009 and keeps ongoing communication with them. Mila wrote about her experiences as an adoptee, about family preservation and ethics, and about her journey through reunion on her retired personal blog, *Yoon's Blur*.

Nikki Mairs-Cayer Pike

Nikki is an adult adoptee of private, domestic (United States), infant adoption. She was born in Maine, an open-access state, and obtained her OBC in December 2009. She has been in reunion with her maternal and paternal original families since January 2010. Nikki is a wife and a mom to both biological and adopted children. She enjoys running, reading and spending time with her family.

Rebecca Hawkes

Rebecca Hawkes is a reunited adult adoptee and a mother to a daughter by birth and a daughter by open adoption from foster care. She lives in Western Massachusetts with her husband and daughters and is a co-founder of ashleysmoms.com. You can read her writings on adoption, family and identity at her blog *Sea Glass & Other Fragments*.

Rosita Gonzalez

Rosita is a transracial, Korean-American adoptee. She is married to a Brit who refers to himself as an Anglo-American and is a mother to two Hapa children. Adopted in 1968 at the age of one, Rosita has not searched for her biological family. Her road has been speckled with Puerto Rican and Appalachian relatives and her biracial sister. While quite content with her role as a "Tennerican," her curiosity has grown recently as her children explore their own ethnic identities. She considers herself a lost daughter, not because of the loss of her birth family, but more because of the loss of her adopted mother, who died in 2001 as Rosita became a first time mother. When she is not supporting her children on their individual paths, Rosita spends her time as an art educator and an art photographer. She also shares her adventures as an adoptee and parent on her blog, *mothermade*.

Samantha Franklin

Samantha is a reunited adoptee (1960s era, closed, private, domestic) from Tulsa, Okla., where she loves life with her husband, Brian, and son, Andrew. She graduated from Oklahoma University with a M.A. in Human Relations and has enjoyed a career in social services and education. She has also served as the Oklahoma Representative for The American Adoption Congress. She has blogged since 2007 about her journey as an adoptee at *Neither Here Nor There*, www.PeachNeitherHereNorThere.blogspot.com.

Stephanie Kripa Cooper-Lewter, Ph.D., L.M.S.W.

Licensed master social worker, speaker, researcher, author, teacher and life coach, Dr. Stephanie Kripa Cooper-Lewter has nearly 20 years of practice experience working in the nonprofit, social service, health, educational and philanthropic sectors addressing a range of family and child welfare issues. She previously served as president/CEO of the Columbia affiliate of Big Brothers Big Sisters of America, the first and youngest Asian-American female to serve in this community leadership role among local United Way certified partner agencies at the time of her service. She earned her Doctorate of Philosophy in Social Work from the University of South Carolina with a Minority Fellowship from the Council on Social Work Education and her Masters of Social Work from the University of Minnesota as a Child Welfare Scholar. Her doctoral dissertation focusing on the life stories of women adopted transnationally as children into white families between the ages of 25-38 and four themes that emerged (difference, connection, identity and the journey), received an Outstanding Dissertation Award from St. John's University Adoption Initiative. She has been active in the adoption community since 1994 when she spoke on her first panel. She has planned numerous adoptee gatherings and serves in leadership roles among several Indian adoptee-led groups including Lost Sarees, Desi Adoptees United, Adopted from India—Missionaries of Charity and Minnesota Adopted Desi. She enjoys spending time with her husband and two children (age 20 and 6) and returned to India in 2009 with her family, traveling to her orphanages and across India. She is also a Certified Personal and Executive Coach and is a graduate of the Coaching and Positive Psychology Institute.

Susan Perry

An adoptee, Susan Perry is the mother of two girls and the grandmother of six. A retired English teacher and public relations professional, she is an active member of the New Jersey Coalition for

Adoption Reform and Education (NJCARE). She has been published in *The Philadelphia Inquirer, The Wall Street Journal* and *PolitickerNJ*, and she regularly advocates for adoption reform at www.nanadays.blogspot.com.

Trace A. DeMeyer

Adoptee Trace A. DeMeyer (Shawnee-Tsalagi-Euro) is an award-winning journalist and the author of *One Small Sacrifice: A Memoir* and the anthology *TWO WORLDS: Lost Children of the Indian Adoption Projects*. Her books are about the history of the Indian Adoption Projects resulting in the Indian Child Welfare Act. Trace is former editor of the *Pequot Times* in Connecticut and editor/co-founder of *Ojibwe Akiing*; she also worked as a reporter at the national Native newspaper *News From Indian Country in Wisconsin*. Her blog is *AMERICAN INDIAN ADOPTEES*. Her website is tracedemeyer.com.

Von

Von is an Australian adoptee of the forced adoption era and has lived the adopted life for almost seven decades. She is known by her family and dearest friends as someone who takes no prisoners and has a horror of bigotry and injustice. She is a strong believer in the rights of children, the power of love, and the medicinal powers of chocolate. She speaks her truth and often describes herself as an adoptee who is "out, proud and loud." She had the benefit of Yorkshire genes for direct speaking and Somerset genes for perseverance. The grandmother in her avatar she never knew but has taken as a role model and an inspiration. She is still waiting to be told she is not the oldest blogger on adoption in the blogosphere. Von blogs regularly at her personal blog, *The Life of Von.*

Made in the USA
Middletown, DE
30 March 2015